龍　虎

鶴麓精舍

# KOREAN
# FOOD
MADE
SIMPLE

# KOREAN FOOD MADE SIMPLE

## JUDY JOO

With Vivian Jao

Photography by Jean Cazals

**HOUGHTON MIFFLIN HARCOURT**

BOSTON NEW YORK 2016

Copyright © 2016 by Judy Joo Media USA Inc.

Food and location photography © 2016 by Jean Cazals

Food styling by Judy Joo and Vivian Jao

Food styling assistance by Cheol Hee Park

Prop styling by Pene Parker

Library of Congress Cataloging-in-Publication Data available upon request.

ISBN 978-0-544-66330-5 (paper over board);

978-0-544-66308-4 (ebook)


Design by Gary Tooth/Empire Design Studio

Printed in China

C&C 10 9 8 7 6 5 4 3 2 1

*Dedicated to my mom, dad, and Sonya, for being the best family I could ever ask for. Thank you for being there for me, no matter what. I love you so much.*

# ACKNOWLEDGMENTS

I have so many people to thank for helping me get through this tricky journey of life, and this book! I love you all, and feel so fortunate to have such amazing people in my life.

First and foremost, my dear mentor, boss, and friend Vivian Jao. Thank you for kicking my butt to get this all done and for making sure it was tested to your first-class standard. You have taught me so much professionally and personally. You are the best.

Thank you, Kathy Brennan, for your meticulous eye in the editing and for your warm smiles.

Annie Woo—I thank you for your friendship and Korean language tutorials and counsel.

Jean Cazals—thank you for your vision and for taking the most beautiful photos of my food I could ever imagine, and braving MERS with me!

Lucia Cho—thank you so much for everything. The beautiful plates from Kwangjuyo, the help with planning the Korea shoot, and most of all your friendship. You and your family have been so wonderful. I love you like a sister.

Han Song—thank you for your gorgeous Troa designs for me to wear. You are so incredibly talented.

Thank you to Cait Hoyt and Justin Schwartz for creating this opportunity for me.

Andy Hales and Jaime Garbutt—you two are my rock and right-hand men. I could not have done any of this without you. I owe you so much. Thank you for supporting me through everything—the blood, sweat, and tears, literally. I love you both

dearly. Thank you, Emma and Steph, too—behind every great man, I know there is an even greater woman. May the adventure continue. . . . I never thought it would go this far!

Janice Gabriel—thank you for being like a surrogate mother to me in London. You were the first person to put me on TV, and I credit my media career to your coaching, mentoring, love, and encouragement. I would not have accomplished so much without your guidance and belief in me. Thank you.

Colman Andrews, Simone Zanoni, Mark Askew, Jason Atherton, and Geoffrey Zakarian—thank you for giving me a chance and the opportunity to work for you and inspiring me. Colman—you have mentored me through the years, and your sage advice has been much appreciated. Thank you for watching over me. Simone, Mark, and Jason—thank you for taking a chance on me, and showing me that with hard work anything is achievable. Geoffrey—your friendship and guiding light has helped me tremendously. Thank you for always being positive and for all your encouragement.

To Kia and Tati Joorabchian—thank you for "opening a window" when a door had just closed. You are like family to me. I am grateful for the opportunity you have provided to me and love you both with all my heart.

And to my amazing friends . . .

Peggy, Karen, Susanne, Nicole, Jen, Jennifer, Laura, Fiona, Vivien, Lorraine, Nigma, Joyce, Ching, Kay, Jen, Sujean, Jean, Amy, Ricker, Judy, Julie-Anne, Cynthia, Yuri, Angie, Jean, Wook, Tony, Elizabeth, Sonny, Craig, Kris, Signe, "E", Steve, Hert, The Taranissi family, Eugene & Jim, Brian, Scott, Sara, Jane, Lynne, and Mark. Without your undying love and support, I wouldn't be here today. Thank you for carrying me during the worst of times and celebrating with me during the best.

A big thank you to H-Mart, www.hmart.com, for sponsoring my book so generously and sharing a vision to bring Korean food to the masses. Thank you in particular to Min Seo and Tony Woo for believing in me and your support.

I also would like to thank wholeheartedly Kia Motors, www.kia.co.uk, for their support with the best ride in town. Hats off to Stephen Kitson and Sara Robinson for making it all happen and being so absolutely amazing to work with.

Thank you as well to Ramy Sal and the Korean Tourism Organization, www.visitkorea.or.kr for supporting my trip to Korea enabling me to bring this tome to life.

Thank you to the Conrad Hotel in Seoul—Nils-Arne Schroeder, you are the best!

Thank you to Andrew Oh and Yoon Jung Choi for your generous hospitality at the Paradise Hotel in Busan. I cannot thank you enough.

# CONTENTS

# INTRODUCTION

Food has always been a big part of my life. Being born into a rather food-obsessed family, with a mother who took the time to cook everything from scratch, I was constantly surrounded by authentic home-cooked Korean food as a child.

Our back porch showcased half a dozen clay pots (*onggi*) with fermenting delights inside, everything from kimchi to *gochujang* to *doenjang*. The laundry room teemed with jars and containers stacked precariously, filled with fermenting drinks, bowls full of soaking tripe, mung beans, bean sprouts, or rice. The adjoining garage had rows of drying seaweed on hangers, chiles, and a small foil-wrapped charcoal grill for barbecue perched in the corner. Even family hiking trips often turned into impromptu foraging ventures, with my mom always on the lookout for wild garlic, bracken root, and chives.

My sister and I were often enlisted to help in this effort to get a taste of home so far from home. Mountains of bean sprouts had to be picked, hundreds of dumplings stuffed, perilla leaves (*ggaennip*) gathered from our garden, and towers of seaweed brushed with oil and toasted. It was all part of my daily life, and my memories surrounding food run deep.

I was born in Summit, New Jersey, and grew up in the modest suburb of Berkeley Heights. My father, a North Korean war refugee, immigrated to the United States in 1967, along with most of his graduating class from Seoul National University College of Medicine. My mom, from Icheon, a city just outside of Seoul, immigrated to the United States on her own in 1968 after being awarded a scholarship to obtain a master's degree in chemistry from Ohio State University. My parents met and married in the States and eventually moved to the East Coast where I was born. I had a typical "tiger mother" upbringing, with all the torturous piano lessons that came with it. I was on a typical Asian fast track to "achieve" and eventually found my way to Columbia University and then to Wall Street, where I sold fixed income derivatives for a number of years. I must admit, it was a fun time in my life. My friends and I ripped around New York City, with a bit of cash in hand, single, working hard and playing even harder. But something was missing. . . . I realized I didn't love my job. It was merely a means to an end. And so the soul-searching began.

I always felt the lure of cooking, but didn't necessarily think that I could become a chef, per se. Nonetheless, after having an epiphany, I took the plunge and quit my fancy Wall Street job to embark on a culinary journey. I duly enrolled in cooking school at the French Culinary Institute (now the International Culinary Center) in New York and then went on to work in the industry in various capacities. Fast-forward a bit, and I became an "Iron Chef" for the U.K. I host my own cooking show, *Korean Food Made Simple*, and I have become a regular face on Food Network. More recently, I've opened my own restaurant in London and Hong Kong, "Jinjuu," where I'm the Chef Patron.

I never really thought any of the prior was possible. Certainly not when you start "late" in the industry. But it just goes to show that a bit of hard work and dedication can take you anywhere.

In this book, you'll find many modern Korean-influenced recipes. I am a French-trained Korean American Londoner, and the different influences in my life show up in my cooking. I grew to love Mexican food while living in California, and the flavors blend well with those found in Korean cuisine. Using matzo meal in my fried chicken seems very natural to me, being a New Yorker. Plus, dishes such as disco fries are a nod to my time growing up in Jersey and eating in the diners off the highways. I also was specifically trained in pastry arts, so you'll see a lot of my classic French training reflected in the sweets chapter. Although I do like traditional Korean desserts, I find that they do not translate well to the Western palate. Traditional Korean ingredients, however, do prove to meld beautifully in classic Western desserts.

Some recipes harbor a bit of a "cheffy" element and others are quite simple, rustic and easy for anyone to do. Regardless, I hope you try and learn to love the flavors of Korea, and incorporate a few Korean ingredients into your everyday cooking.

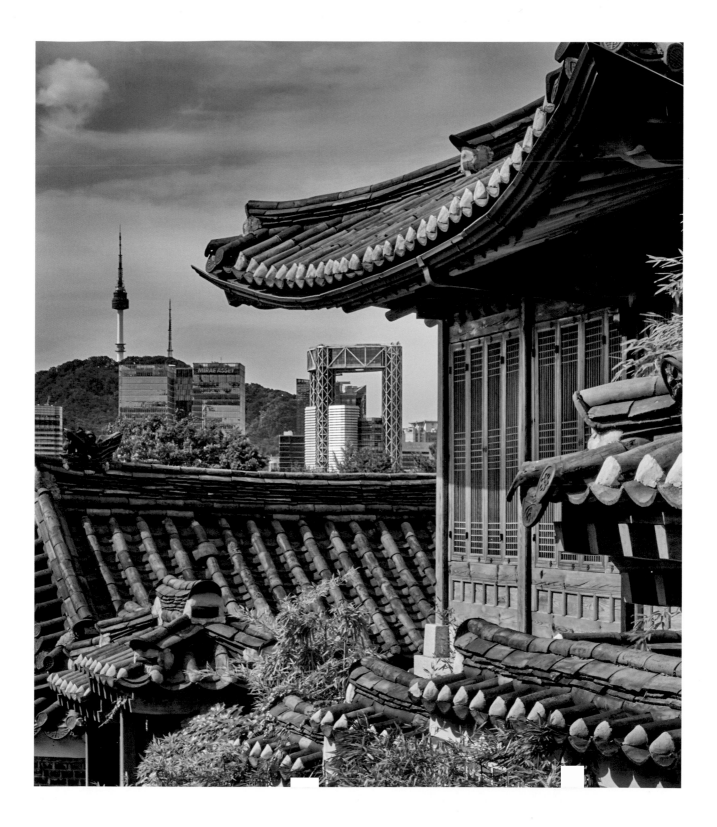

Tiny Dried Anchovies

Salted Shrimp

*Doenjang*
(Korean Soybean Paste)

Large Dried
Anchovies

Rice Cake ¨Ovalettes¨

*Gochujang*
(Korean Chile Paste)

Cylindrical Rice Cakes

Citron Tea Syrup

# THE KOREAN PANTRY

There are a number of staple items necessary to successfully
embark on a journey of Korean cooking.

### Asian Pears (*Bae*)

Asian pears, also called Nashi or apple pears, are
one of the sweetest and most popular fruits in
Korea. Round like an apple, but texturally like a
crisp pear, these large fruits are ambrosial and
delectably juicy. The most famous ones are from
the southern town of Naju, and these varieties
can grow as big as melons. Eaten fresh or used to
marinate meats, or even in kimchi, these pears
are wonderfully versatile.

### Brown Seaweed (*Miyuk*)

*Miyuk* is a dried seaweed that is considerably
thicker than *kim* (see page 23) but thinner than
*kombu* or *dashima*. Like *kombu*, it comes in long
packages, but it's texturally much more wrinkly
and twisted in appearance. It can also be found
precut into strips, and expands greatly as it soaks
in liquid. *Miyuk* is used for soups, especially the
famous birthday Seaweed Soup (page 139).

### Citron Tea Syrup (*Yujacha*)

This marmalade-like citron syrup or "honey" is
most often used for making tea. Technically, it
is not citron but *yuja*, known as yuzu in Japan, a
fragrant and floral citrus fruit that tastes something like a lemon crossed with a tangerine. I use
this for tea as well as in a number of desserts and
savory dishes.

### *Doenjang* (Korean Soybean Paste)

This dark brown and richly flavored paste is made
from fermented soybeans, and has a 2,000 year
history. It is coarser (often contains whole beans)
and stronger in flavor than its Japanese counterpart, miso. The soybeans are boiled, pressed into
blocks called meju, and then hung to dry using
dried rice stalks, which are rich in bacteria
(bacillus subtilis) that starts the fermentation
process. Once the meju is fermented and dried
enough (depending on the size, up to 50 days), the
blocks are placed in salted water and allowed to
ferment further, for up to 6 months. Once the
process is complete, the liquid is drained off—this
is used to make soy sauce. The remaining bean
pulp is then made into *doenjang*. This paste has a
deep, rich, salty flavor that goes a long way in soup,
stews, marinades, and dressings.

### Dried Anchovies (*Myulchi*)

Dried anchovies come in several sizes. Use the
large ones for making broth, removing the head
and innards beforehand. The tiny and smaller
ones are stir-fried with honey and soy and other
flavorings to make Crispy Anchovies (page 72) for
a very tasty *banchan* (side dishes).

### Dried Black Soybeans (*Seoritae*)

Korean black soybeans are the base for another
fundamental *banchan* side dish, *kongjorim*. Sweet
and salty, this side is surprisingly addictive.

### Dried Chile Threads (*Silgochu*)

These intricate fiery threads look much like
saffron, but are longer and more wiry. Made from
thinly sliced chiles, *silgochu* add a dramatic colorful
touch as a garnish, as well as a bit of heat.

### Dried Kelp (*Dashima*)

*Dashima*, also known as *kombu*, are dried sheets of
kelp, and are often used with dried anchovies to

make a classic Korean stock. This base makes for an umami-filled, rich broth that tastes of the sea. It is akin to chicken broth in the West, and my mom even uses this tasty stock instead of water to add to her kimchi.

### Dried Shiitake Mushrooms (*Pyogo Beoseot*)

Add shiitake mushrooms to *dashima* broth and you'll have an even more umami-infused, rich broth.

### Fresh Korean Chiles, Red and Green (*Gochu*)

Korean chiles have evolved into their own species, and are closely related to the Thai chile. Ironically, the much-loved chile is not indigenous to Korea, but was introduced to the country in 1615 via Portuguese missionaries traveling with Japanese troops. Red or green in color, they are medium-spicy and used fresh, dried, and powdered. Koreans love a bit of spice in their food.

### Garlic (*Manul*)

Garlic is a staple ingredient in Korean cooking. It is eaten both cooked and raw and used in everything from kimchi to barbecue marinades to dipping sauces. It adds a punchy hit of flavor and is full of antioxidants. I use so much garlic that I often just buy the pre-peeled fresh cloves from the refrigerator section at the grocery store. My favorite quick way to "mince" garlic is to grate it on a microplane.

### Gochugaru (Korean Chile Flakes)

This staple ingredient is made from dried Korean chiles. Traditionally sun-dried, deseeded, and then crushed, this staple chile flake is used ubiquitously in Korean cooking and is an essential ingredient in many dishes, including Korea's national dish,

kimchi. It comes in several varieties: mild to spicy, and coarse or fine. I like to stock up on vibrant red, medium spicy, coarse flakes. I use it as my go-to chile to sprinkle on top of everything from pizza to veggies. Store it in an airtight container in your freezer to keep it fresh and its pungency intact.

### Gochujang (Korean Chile Paste)

This fiery red chile paste is most commonly made from *gochugaru* (Korean chile flakes), dried fermented soybean powder (*meju garu*), sweet rice powder, and salt. Sometimes honey or sugar is added as well. After this paste has been left to ferment, the richness and complexity of the flavor comes out and makes for a uniquely Korean chile experience. It is used throughout Korean cooking and is completely versatile. Use it right out of the box or cook it down; it doesn't matter. This paste can be used in anything you want to give a little spice, and serious flavor.

### Jujubes (*Daechu*)

Jujubes are dried Chinese red dates, often used to flavor soups, teas, or desserts. They taste more reserved, not as sweet or sticky as Deglet Noor or Medjool dates.

### Kimchi

No meal in Korea is complete without kimchi on the table. Currently, there are officially 187 different varieties of kimchi, and the average Korean consumes about 40 kilograms (about 88 pounds) of it a year. This national dish is made from seasoned and usually brined vegetables that are then left to ferment. This fermentation process creates a notable

Jujubes

Buckwheat-Sweet Potato Noodles

Roasted Seaweed

Korean Hot Mustard

*Gochugaru* (Korean chile flakes)

Julienned Roasted Seaweed

Dried Chile Threads

Black Soybeans

Dried kelp

Sweet Potato Noodles

Brown Seaweed (Precut)

Mung Bean Sprouts

Napa

Daikon

Soybean Sprouts

Lotus Root

Perilla Leaves

Korean Sweet Potato

Green Chile

Twist Peppers

Asian Pear

Red Chile

complex flavor that incorporates spice, tang, sweetness, and an addictive crispy texture. The best-known variety is made from Korean cabbages or napa cabbage. Kimchi is most often eaten raw, but you'll find it incorporated into soups, stews, and stir-fries, and the liquid, or kimchi juice, can even be used to make a killer Spiced Kimchi Mary (page 271).

### Korean Hot Mustard (*Gyeoja*)

Korean yellow mustard is hot and spicy, much like English mustard such as Colman's. It comes in both powdered and prepared forms (in tubes). As the prepared versions can vary greatly in their spiciness, I prefer to use the powder for my dressings and marinades.

### Korean Napa Cabbage (*Baechu*)

Korean napa cabbage is the main ingredient in kimchi. Napa cabbage is longer and leafier than its round, hard Western counterpart. The napa variety found in Korean stores is also much larger than those found in regular grocery stores. Korean napa are huge and usually about 5 pounds each. Look for crisp leaves (not wilted), a firm head, and unblemished white ribs. When preparing, be sure to remove the tough outer leaves.

### Korean Radish (*Mu*)

Korean radish is large, greenish, and fat, unlike its long, skinny, white counterpart, the daikon or mouli radish. It has a lower water content, too, so the flesh feels denser and has a slightly spicier taste as well. You can substitute daikon if you cannot find Korean radish. Use in soups and stews and for making kimchi.

### Korean Sweet Potato (*Goguma*)

Korean sweet potatoes have reddish skin and whitish flesh. They are sweeter and softer than Western sweet potatoes, and a bit longer and knobbier in appearance. In Korea, they are a common street food snack, either simply roasted and served up in brown paper bags or fried into an addictive sugar-coated snack called *mattang*, Candied Sweet Potato Wedges (page 61).

### Korean Vinegar (*Shikcho*)

Korean cooking uses a lot of vinegars, and notably fruit vinegars. Vinegar brings a much-needed astringent taste to Korean cuisine to balance out the other bold flavors. Apple vinegar (*sagwa-shikcho*) and rice vinegar are the most commonly used for cooking. Pomegranate, black raspberry, and persimmon vinegars are quite popular to use in drinks.

### Lotus Root (*Yeongeun*)

All parts of the lotus plant are used in Korean cooking, but the roots are the most common. Resembling the spout of a watering can, the roots are both a gorgeous garnish and tasty addition to many dishes. As a side dish, pickled, candied, or deep-fried, its crunchy texture and mild flavor make it a popular ingredient in many Asian cuisines.

### Mirin

Usually described as a cooking wine, mirin (aka mirim) has a sweet flavor and low alcohol content. It is used in numerous applications in Korean cooking. It's widely available at regular supermarkets, but if you cannot find it, feel free to substitute lemon-lime-flavored soda.

### Mung Beans (*Nokdu*)

Whole mung beans wear a green skin. When the skin is removed and the bean is split, their dark yellow flesh is revealed. Mung beans and their sprouts (*sukju*) are commonly used to make pancakes called *bindaetteok*.

### Perilla Leaves (*Ggaennip*)

Perilla or sesame leaves are not to be confused with the Japanese shiso leaf, which is smaller and more jagged around the edges. Although they are also referred to as sesame leaves, they actually do not come from the sesame plant. Perilla leaves have a slightly minty flavor and are thicker and heartier in texture. They are rounder than shiso leaves and often have a deep-purple fuzzy underside. Use them as *ssam* (wrappers) for meat or make them into a version of kimchi. I like to toss them into salads for a welcome fragrant note or even muddle them into a cocktail.

### Persimmons (*Gam*), Fresh and Dried

There are two kinds of persimmons found in Korea. One is the soft, heart-shaped, astringent "sour" persimmon, *hongsi*, or Hachiya in Japanese. It is quite pulpy and must be ripe before eating. The other is the "sweet," squat, and hard in texture *dan gam* or Fuyu persimmon. It boasts a pumpkinlike flavor and can be eaten like an apple. There is also a popular flat, seedless version of the *hongsi* called *bansi*. Persimmons can be dried and used to make dessert drinks such as *sujeonggwa*, Cinnamon and Persimmon Punch (page 267), or when frozen they can be made into a sorbetlike dessert. They are also used to make wine, vinegar, and cookies.

### Pork Belly

Pork belly is a very popular cut in Korean cooking. It finds its way into stir-fries, soups, and barbecue. Either cut into slabs for *bossam* or *samgyeopsal*, or thinly sliced for *bokkeum* or barbecue, pork belly marries well with Korea's national dish, kimchi, and another staple ingredient, ginger.

### Rice (*Ssal*:raw, *Bap*:cooked)

Many different types of rice are consumed in Korea, but the most popular and prized variety is white short-grain rice. Short-grain rice is fat, roundish, and when cooked the kernels stick together (but not as much as "sticky rice"), giving it a satisfying toothsome quality. Rice symbolizes wealth, purity, and prosperity. White rice, in particular, was the food of the noblemen, while the peasants ate the cheaper brown rice mixed with grains. Korean rice is cooked with just water, and no flavorings are added. It has also been completely stripped of all its nutrients, in favor of a white pearly complexion. It is also very common to mix rice with legumes or other grains such as amaranth, spelt, barley, or oats, as well as other kinds of rice such as black, red, or brown.

### Rice Cakes (*Dduk*)

These dense, cylindrical rice cakes are served in a variety of ways, including in soups (traditionally on New Year's Day), stir-fries, and straight up from the toaster oven. I grew up loving their toothsome, chewy texture. Made from glutinous rice flour, they come in various widths and shapes and are used in both savory and sweet dishes. The cylindrical sticks must be pulled apart before using. They are also often sold sliced into discs called "ova-lettes." Fresh rice cakes are highly perishable and must be used quickly after they are purchased; they can also be thrown in the freezer (wrapped well) for a later use.

### Rice Flour (Ssalgaru)

I use a lot of rice flour to add crispiness to anything fried. If used solo as well, it can keep your meal gluten-free. Note that rice flour and sweet rice flour (aka glutinous rice flour), are not the same and are not interchangeable. Sweet rice flour (chapssalgaru) is ground from glutinous rice and yields a completely different (stickier and chewier) texture and end product. Ironically, despite its name, glutinous rice is gluten free.

### Roasted Seaweed (Kim)

Koreans eat a lot of seaweed in various forms. Kim (or gim) is probably the most popular and can be bought ready-made and used as a wrapper, but differs greatly from nori, its Japanese sister. Kim is much thinner, seasoned delicately with salt, and lightly toasted, giving it a crispy, addictive quality.

### Salt (Sogeum)

Throughout this book, I'm using kosher or sea salt. Korea, however, has a long tradition of artisan salts of numerous varieties. Korean solar salt, cheonilyeom, is particularly fortified with minerals and cultivated in a meticulous way. I also like the aged bamboo salt, jukyeom, of the south. These special salts, however, proved too hard to find to call for in these recipes. If you do find yourself in a Korean grocery store, try to seek them out for a pleasant surprise.

### Salted Shrimp (Saewoo Jeot)

These tiny salted shrimp are mostly used in the making of kimchi, but they are also incorporated into seasoning banchan, soups, and stews. They are very salty, so feel free to rinse and drain well and use sparingly. You'll find the flavor is quite intense, adding serious depth to whatever you add these tiny shrimp to.

### Sesame Seeds (Kkae)

Koreans use sesame seeds (both black and white) in copious amounts. The white variety is more common, and you can buy sesame seeds preroasted and crushed in Asian grocery stores. If you can't find them preroasted, a quick toast in a skillet or oven will do the trick as well. Use them as a garnish and in dipping sauces to enhance the flavor with a bit of crunchy texture. I like to use a mix of whole and ground seeds for a contrast of textures, both visually and to the bite.

### Short Ribs (Galbi)

Beef short ribs are the cornerstone of the famed Korean barbecue. Sliced either along the ribs, L.A. cut, or thinly sliced around the bone, this nicely marbled cut is tender and full of flavor. Blocks cut between the bones are used for stews that are cooked until the rich meat pulls away easily from the ribs.

### Soju

Although soju is commonly referred to as Korea's rice wine, it is actually not a wine. Soju is a distilled spirit more similar to vodka than sake. In its purest form it is made from just rice and water. It is also the most consumed alcohol in the world, which gives you an idea as to how much Koreans drink!

### Soy Sauce (*Ganjang*)

Another fermented product, soy sauce is the by-product of making *doenjang*. There are many different kinds with various uses. Dark soy sauce is used for heartier dishes, while the lighter variety is used for seasoning vegetables. Throughout this book, just use regular soy sauce, as the different varieties can be hard to find. Naturally-aged soy sauces are the best, but can be expensive. The older and higher-quality the soy sauce, the richer and deeper the flavor—think umami.

### Soybean Sprouts (*Kong Namul*) and Mung Bean Sprouts (*Sukju Namul*)

Soybean sprouts are served in everything from soups to *banchan*. They have a large, yellow, crunchy heads, skinny whitish stems, and a long roots that should be snipped off. Soybean sprouts are slightly sweet and have a great firm texture even when cooked. The bright yellow heads are the best part. They are a vital ingredient in many soups and stews and a very popular and healthy *banchan*.

Greenish mung beans produce sprouts that have small, unremarkable heads and fatter, watery stems. Mung bean sprouts are most commonly used in *banchan*, pancakes, and salads.

### Sweet Potato Noodles (*Dangmyun*)

Naturally gluten-free, these glass noodles have a truly satisfying stretchy, chewy texture and are used mainly for *japchae*. They have little flavor on their own, but they soak up any sauce nicely.

### Toasted Sesame Oil (*Chamgireum*)

This earthy oil is used as a flavoring rather than to cook with. Made from roasted and ground sesame seeds, it has a unique nutty aroma and rich distinguishable flavor. A little goes a long way, and sometimes a quick drizzle is all you need to give a dish that final flourishing touch of finesse. When purchasing, make sure you buy 100% pure sesame oil as there are many cheaper blends that are quite muddled in taste.

### Tofu (*Dubu*), Silken, Soft, Medium, Firm

Koreans love the soybean in all forms, and tofu (*dubu*) is no exception. It is considered a staple source of protein and is eaten with or without meat. It is a food in its own right and not considered a vegetarian-only ingredient. Also known as bean curd, tofu is made from pressing soy milk curds mixed with a coagulant into blocks. There are numerous varieties, but the main types are silken, soft, medium, and firm. Silken tofu is the softest due to its high water content. It is used mostly in stews and in the West as a dairy substitute. Soft, medium, and firm tofu are named according to their firmness, the result of the amount of draining and pressing each type has gone through. Use the type of tofu that best suits your needs without it falling apart easily.

### Twist Peppers (*Gwari*)

These wrinkled smallish green peppers (*shishito* in Japan) are mild in flavor. They are good for pickling with soy sauce, eaten fresh with *doenjang*, or simply grilled.

Bone-in L.A. Cut
Beef Short Ribs

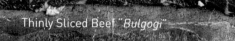
Thinly Sliced Beef "*Bulgogi*"

Boneless Skin-on Pork Belly

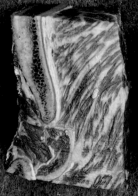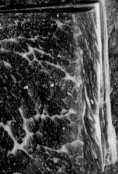
Beef Short Ribs

# KIMCHI &
# PICKLES

# CABBAGE KIMCHI

*POGI KIMCHI*

**MAKES ABOUT 1 GALLON**

Aside from barbecue, kimchi is probably the dish most synonymous with Korean cuisine. This fiery red, funky, fermented cabbage is on the table every meal—breakfast, lunch, and dinner, 365 days a year. It is one of the cornerstones of Korean cooking, and Koreans consider it vital to their daily diet. This recipe is an adaptation of the one we use at my restaurant, Jinjuu. Kimchi making may look daunting, but don't worry, it's really very straightforward. You'll just need to have one or two very large bowls for the brining of the cabbage and a large container to ferment it in. Also, I highly recommend that you wear plastic or latex gloves while smearing the chile paste onto the cabbage leaves. Otherwise, your hands will be tingling afterward and the odor, while delicious, will linger on your skin.

Many Korean households purchase premade kimchi these days, and you can certainly do that and use it wherever kimchi is called for in my recipes, but please do try making this at least once.

8 cups warm water

1½ cups kosher salt or coarse sea salt

1 very large Korean cabbage or several heads napa cabbage (5 to 6 pounds total), bottom(s) trimmed, wilted and tough outer leaves discarded, and rinsed well

2 small onions, coarsely chopped

12 dried shiitake mushrooms

10 large dried anchovies (*myulchi*), head and guts removed

6 scallions, coarsely chopped

64 cloves garlic, 8 crushed and the rest left whole

1 (10-inch-long) piece dried kelp (*dashima*)

2½ cups *gochugaru* (Korean chile flakes)

14 tablespoons fish sauce

10 tablespoons salted shrimp (*saewoo jeot*), rinsed

4 tablespoons sugar

1 (7-inch) knob fresh ginger, peeled and chopped

3 carrots, julienned

12 scallions, cut into 2-inch pieces

7 ounces Korean white radish (*mu*) or daikon, peeled and julienned

IN A LARGE BOWL, stir together the warm water and ¾ cup of the salt until the salt has dissolved; let the salted water cool. Meanwhile, partially cut the cabbage(s) in half lengthwise, starting from the root end and cutting about halfway to the top. Using your hands, pull the cabbage(s) apart to split in half completely. Repeat so that each half is halved in the same way, which keeps the leaves intact and whole.

Loosen the leaves of each wedge so that they are easy to spread. Sprinkle the remaining ¾ cup salt over and between all the leaves, salting the core area more heavily. Put the cabbage into a large bowl (use two if they don't fit) cut-side up. Pour the cooled salted water over the cabbage, then

pour enough cold water into the bowl to cover the cabbage; don't overfill the bowl, as some liquid will be drawn out of the cabbage. Weigh down the cabbage with a plate so the wedges are completely immersed. Let sit at room temperature for 6 to 8 hours, flipping the wedges halfway through.

Rinse the wedges well under cold running water and gently squeeze out any excess moisture. Put the wedges cut side down in a colander and let drain for at least 30 minutes.

Meanwhile, in a small saucepan, combine the onions, mushrooms, anchovies, scallions, the 8 crushed garlic cloves, and the kelp and bring to a boil over high heat. Reduce the heat to maintain a simmer for 20 minutes. Strain the liquid, discarding the solids, and let the anchovy stock cool completely.

When the stock has cooled, in a food processor, combine the remaining garlic cloves, chile flakes, fish sauce, salted shrimp, sugar, and ginger and process until smooth. Add enough of the stock to make a smooth paste, about 2 cups total. Discard any remaining stock. Transfer the spice paste to a large bowl and stir in the carrots, scallions, and radish.

Rub the spice paste all over the cabbage wedges and between each leaf. Pull the outermost leaf of each wedge tightly over the rest of the wedge, forming a tidy package. Pack the wedges into one or more glass or other nonreactive containers with a tight-fitting lid (see Tip, below). Press a piece of plastic wrap directly on the surface of the kimchi, then cover. The kimchi can be eaten at this young stage or after it sits at room temperature and starts to get sour and "bubble," 2 to 3 days. Store the kimchi in the refrigerator, where it will continue to ferment at a slower pace. I like to age mine at least 2 weeks, but it really is up to preference. Cut the kimchi before serving.

TIP: *While large glass jars or Korean earthenware containers are preferred for storing kimchi, they're not always easy to find. Look in the housewares section of Korean markets for glass or plastic kimchi containers, which have become popular. You can also use any sturdy BPA-free plastic or other nonreactive container with a tight-fitting lid. You'll need a container or containers with a total capacity of 1 gallon for the kimchi.*

# CUBED RADISH KIMCHI

## *KKAKDUGI*

### MAKES ABOUT 2 QUARTS

*Kkakdugi* is probably my favorite of all kimchis due to its serious crunch factor and the addition of rice flour, which gives the sauce a nice thickness and body. This recipe was shared by Young Sook Kim of River Edge, New Jersey, who makes it both for family and in huge quantities for her church fundraisers. I first tried it at my friend and co-author, Vivian Jao's house, and when I couldn't stop eating it, I just had to have the recipe.

Korean white radish and daikon are often interchangeable in recipes, but for this recipe, it's important to use the former. Daikon will soften too much and not hold up as well. If your radish is very fresh and smooth skinned, there's no need peel it. Just scrub it well and remove any blemished spots.

3 pounds Korean white radish (*mu*) (about 1 large), peeled and cut into ¾-to 1-inch cubes

2 tablespoons kosher salt or coarse sea salt

1 tablespoon sweet rice flour

⅓ red bell pepper, seeded and chopped

¼ small onion, chopped

5 cloves garlic

2 fresh Korean red chiles or Fresno chiles, chopped (optional)

3 tablespoons *gochugaru* (Korean chile flakes)

2 teaspoons salted shrimp (*saewoo jeot*), rinsed

2 teaspoons fish sauce

2 teaspoons sugar, or ⅛ Asian or other firm but ripe pear, peeled and chopped

1 (¾-inch) knob fresh ginger, peeled and sliced

3 scallions, cut into ¼-inch pieces

IN A LARGE BOWL, toss together the radish and salt. Let sit for about an hour, stirring every 15 minutes. Meanwhile, in a small saucepan, stir together 6 tablespoons water and the sweet rice flour. Cook over medium heat, stirring often, until it thickens and starts to bubble, 4 to 5 minutes. Transfer the flour mixture to a medium bowl and let cool to room temperature.

In a food processor, combine the bell pepper, onion, garlic, red chiles, chile flakes, shrimp, fish

Cubed Radish Kimchi
(page 31)

Cubed Pickled Radish
(page 34)

Spicy Pickled Radish Salad
(page 34)

sauce, sugar, and ginger and process until smooth. Scrape the chile mixture into the cooled flour mixture, add the scallions, and mix well. The resulting spice mixture should taste slightly salty (the saltiness will go away once properly fermented). It must have a certain saltiness so it ferments properly, otherwise the radish will rot at the core and go soft.

Add the spice mixture to the radish mixture, keeping any liquid in the bowl, and mix well. Transfer to a clean half-gallon glass jar or other nonreactive container, packing it in firmly. Cover tightly and let the kimchi sit in a cool place for about 24 hours or at room temperature for about 16 hours. Refrigerate for 3 to 7 days more before

serving (Young Sook prefers to wait a full week so the kimchi develops a stronger flavor). If at any point during the process, you see the juices bubbling and ready to overflow, open the jar and push the radish down to let the gas out. Try not to let any juice escape from the jar. The radish should be completely submerged.

TIP: *Young Sook has some rules for her* kkakdugi *that applies to pretty much all kimchi: try not to open the jar too often. Only remove the amount you will eat at that time. Never transfer to another container and leave it there for more than a day because the flavor will change and the kimchi will taste "off."*

# CUBED PICKLED RADISH

## *DANMUJI OR CHICKEN MU*

**MAKES ABOUT 1 QUART**

Any reputable Korean fried chicken joint will provide these refreshing sweet pickles to offset their fried offerings. Some people like to include lemon-lime soda when pickling, but I don't think it needs it. It's an essential accompaniment to Ultimate KFC (Korean Fried Chicken, page 167). We serve this pickle at Jinjuu, and customers are always asking for more.

½ cup rice vinegar

½ cup superfine sugar

1 teaspoon kosher salt or sea salt

1 pound Korean white radish (*mu*) or daikon, peeled and cut into ½-inch cubes

Pinch of black sesame seeds, for serving (optional)

IN A LARGE BOWL, stir together the vinegar, sugar, salt, and ½ cup water until the sugar and salt have dissolved. Add the radish and toss to coat. Cover and let marinate at room temperature for about 24 hours, then refrigerate. Sprinkle with the sesame seeds when serving.

# SPICY PICKLED RADISH SALAD

## *MUSAENGCHE*

**MAKES ABOUT 1½ CUPS**

The slender shape of julienned radish makes for quick pickling. This easy radish salad hits both the fiery notes of red kimchi and the sweetness of pickled radish. It's great for your *banchan* spread or as a burst of freshness tucked into a Roasted Pork Belly Lettuce Wrap (page 200) or Doenjang-Glazed Lamb Lettuce Wrap (page 194). Try it on sandwiches as well, in lieu of pickled hot peppers or jalapeño slices.

6 ounces Korean white radish (*mu*) or daikon, peeled and julienned

1½ tablespoons Korean apple vinegar (*sagwa-shikcho*) or rice vinegar

1½ tablespoons sugar

1½ teaspoons *gochugaru* (Korean chile flakes)

1 small clove garlic, grated or minced

1 teaspoon kosher salt or sea salt

IN A MEDIUM BOWL, stir together all the ingredients until the radish is coated. Cover and refrigerate for about 1 hour before serving.

# CUCUMBER KIMCHI

*OI KIMCHI*

**MAKES ABOUT 1 QUART**

One of the most beloved versions of kimchi takes a bit of time, but you'll be pleasantly surprised by the results. This kimchi tastes great on top of my Krazy Korean Burgers (page 185) as well, as a different take on the American pickle.

1 pound small Korean cucumbers (*oi*)
or Kirbies (about 4 total)

1 tablespoon kosher salt or sea salt

1 onion, coarsely chopped

4 scallions, chopped

1 tablespoon *gochugaru* (Korean chile flakes)

1 tablespoon salted shrimp
(*saewoo jeot*), rinsed

1 small clove garlic

1 (1-inch) knob fresh ginger,
peeled and chopped

15 fresh chives, cut into 2-inch pieces

USING A SMALL KNIFE, cut each cucumber cross-wise into 2-inch pieces. Stand the pieces on their cut sides and cut each one two-thirds of the way down into quarters, keeping them attached at the bottom. Sprinkle the cucumbers with the salt, spreading the cucumbers open to get the salt deep inside the cuts. Arrange the cucumbers with their cross cut sides up in a single layer in a glass or other nonreactive container, at least 2 inches tall, with a tight-fitting lid, cover, and let soften at room temperature for 30 minutes to 1 hour.

Meanwhile, in a food processor, combine the onion, scallions, chile flakes, shrimp, garlic, ginger, and 2 tablespoons water. Pulse until a coarse spice paste forms and then stir in the chives.

Rinse the salted cucumbers well under cold water, making sure to rid the crevices of all the salt. Shake dry and then press the spice paste all over and into the crevices of each piece. Return the cucumbers to the (rinsed) container, cross cut sides up, packing them somewhat tightly and pressing in any remaining spice paste and liquid. Cover and let the cucumbers ferment at room temperature for about 24 hours. Refrigerate until ready to serve.

# PERILLA (AKA SESAME) LEAF KIMCHI

## *GGAENNIP KIMCHI*

**MAKES 50 LEAVES**

Korean perilla leaves are commonly called sesame leaves, although they have no relation to the sesame plant. Perilla leaves are part of the mint family and are related to the more delicate Japanese shiso leaf. If you're a fan of mint and basil, you'll probably like perilla leaves. They're very easy to grow from seeds, both in the ground and in pots. In fact, much like mint, they grow like weeds and can be invasive. If you let one of the plants go to seed, you'll be sure to have more plants sprouting up in the spring. My mom used to grow it in our garden by the bushel. I got so sick and tired of picking it, that I wouldn't eat it for many years. Its kimchi version, however, persuaded me to love it again.

Include this kimchi as part of your *banchan* spread or use the leaves like roasted seaweed and wrap around a mouthful of rice.

50 perilla leaves (*ggaennip*), also known
as sesame leaves

¼ cup julienned onion

¼ cup julienned carrot

5 cloves garlic, grated or minced

2 scallions, thinly sliced on an angle

2 tablespoons *gochugaru* (Korean chile flakes)

2 tablespoons toasted sesame oil

1 tablespoon fish sauce

1 tablespoon soy sauce

1 tablespoon roasted sesame seeds

1 tablespoon honey

HOLD THE PERILLA LEAVES by the stems and rinse each leaf well under running water. Shake off any excess water and set in a colander to drain.

In a small bowl, stir together the onion, carrot, garlic, scallions, chile flakes, sesame oil, fish sauce, soy sauce, sesame seeds, honey, and 2 table-spoons water. Spread some of this paste on the bottom of a glass or other nonreactive container with a tight-fitting lid that is wide enough to fit a leaf lying flat and tall enough to fit all the leaves stacked together. Lay a stack of 2 or 3 perilla leaves on the paste and spread some more paste on the top leaf. Stack another 2 or 3 leaves on top and spread more paste on the top leaf. Continue until all the leaves have been used.

Spread any remaining sauce on top of the leaves and then press down on them to force out any air. The leaves can be eaten right away or refrigerated, covered, for up to a week. They can be eaten as a side dish or as a wrapper with rice. The yield will vary depending on how long you refrigerate it. It's a nice tall stack when first prepared, but then wilts down considerably the longer it sits.

TIP: *Some people like to blanch larger, tougher perilla leaves before pickling them. It softens them a bit and mellows their flavor.*

# RADISH WATER KIMCHI

*DONGCHIMI*

**MAKES ABOUT 1 GALLON**

Unlike its fiery red brethren, water kimchi (*mul kimchi*) is a light refreshing kimchi in a clear watery broth. Sometimes a little *gochugaru* is added to make the broth reddish in color and give it a little heat. Or sometimes sliced chiles or whole chiles that have been pricked to release their flavor are added to give a gentle spiciness.

*Dongchimi* is a specific type of mul kimchi that is usually made in the wintertime. It is served as a chilled soup, and the tart and refreshing brine-based broth makes it perfect for a hot summer day. Use this broth also to add to Ice-Cold Noodles (*Naengmyun*, page 119). Water kimchi is also one of the easier and faster kimchis to prepare, so don't hesitate to try it. As with Cubed Radish Kimchi (page 31), be sure to use Korean radishes in this recipe so it will hold up to the lengthy pickling time. If your radish is very fresh and smooth skinned, there's no need to peel it. Just scrub it well and remove any blemished spots.

3 pounds (about 1 large) Korean white radish (*mu*), quartered lengthwise and rinsed briefly

4 tablespoons kosher salt or sea salt

3 tablespoons sugar

1 carrot, peeled and thinly sliced on an angle

1 small Asian pear or other firm but ripe pear, quartered and cored

6 scallions, cut into 2-inch-long pieces

6 cloves garlic

3 fresh Korean red chiles or Fresno chiles, pricked in several spots

3 fresh Korean green chiles or jalapeños, pricked in several spots

1 (1-inch) knob fresh ginger, peeled and thinly sliced

PUT THE RADISH in a large, wide, shallow bowl, sprinkle with 2 tablespoons of the salt and 1 tablespoon of the sugar, and roll the radish until evenly coated on all sides. Cover and let sit at room temperature for 8 hours or up to 1 day.

Transfer the radish to a 1-gallon glass or other nonreactive container with a tight-fitting lid, reserving any liquid. Add the carrot, pear, scallions, garlic, red and green chiles, and ginger.

In a medium bowl, combine the remaining 2 tablespoons salt, 2 tablespoons sugar, and 2 cups warm water and stir until the salt and sugar have dissolved. Stir in 4 cups cold water.

Pass the reserved radish liquid through a fine-mesh strainer into the bowl of brine. The brine should taste just a little salty, but not overly so. Add a little more salt to taste or water to dilute, if needed. Pour the brine over the radish mixture in the container, making sure you leave enough space at the top for the gasses that will be released. Cover and let ferment at room temperature until you see bubbles forming and the brining liquid tastes tart, 1 to 2 days. Refrigerate until ready to serve.

To serve, take a piece of radish, cut it into thin slices, and fan it out in a bowl. If you'd like, garnish with some of the carrots and chiles from the container. Pour some of the brining liquid into the bowl and dilute with chilled water to taste.

*TIP: There are two other versions of this kimchi which involve the same basic recipe but with different radish shapes and fermenting times. One involves cutting the radish into 2 x ½-inch sticks. The smaller size allows it to ferment faster. The initial salting takes only about an hour and the bubbles will start forming faster, too. The other side of the spectrum is using small radishes, small enough to fit into the container whole. Unlike the sticks, these take at least a full day to salt and even longer to ferment, but they stay fresh longer.*

# PANCAKES,
# DUMPLINGS,
# & OTHER
# SMALL BITES

# POTATO PANCAKES WITH ASIAN PEAR COMPOTE

*GAMJA JEON*

**MAKES ABOUT 10 PANCAKES**

Coming from North-Central New Jersey and New York City, I've been lucky to have had my share of latkes. Traditional Korean potato pancakes are different than Jewish latkes, using a much finer grating of the potatoes, which results in a softer texture. I've brought the two versions together in my Korean take on the classic fried potato pancakes with applesauce. My potato pancakes are crispy and have more potato integrity, but I've included Korean flavors as well as an Asian pear compote in lieu of applesauce. I think it marries the best of both worlds.

I like to use a mixture of russet and Yukon Gold potatoes. The russets provide crispness, while the Yukons have better potato flavor and lend a golden color. I don't peel either type.

Compote:

**1¼ pounds Asian pears or other firm but ripe pears, peeled, cored, and cut into 1-inch pieces**

**2 tablespoons sugar**

**1 tablespoon fresh lemon juice**

**1 (½-inch) knob fresh ginger, peeled and sliced**

**Pinch of kosher salt or sea salt**

Pancakes:

**1 pound russet and Yukon Gold potatoes, unpeeled (any ratio of the two types)**

**1 onion, quartered**

**2 tablespoons potato starch**

**1 tablespoon crushed sesame seeds**

**2 teaspoons *gochugaru* (Korean chile flakes)**

**1 teaspoon *gochujang* (Korean chile paste)**

**1 teaspoon kosher salt or sea salt, plus more for finishing**

**2 large eggs, lightly beaten**

**Vegetable oil, for frying**

**FOR THE COMPOTE:** In a small saucepan, combine all the compote ingredients and 2 tablespoons water and bring to a boil over medium-high heat, stirring until the sugar has dissolved. Reduce the heat to maintain a simmer, stirring occasionally, until the fruit mashes easily with the back of a fork, about 20 minutes. Remove from the heat, discard the ginger, and mash the mixture into a chunky sauce. (If you prefer a smooth sauce, puree the mixture in a food processor.) Set aside.

**FOR THE PANCAKES:** In a food processor fitted with the medium grating disc, shred the potatoes and onion quarters, alternating between the two (the onion juices help keep the potatoes from discoloring). Alternatively, grate the potatoes and onion on the large holes of a box grater.

Working in batches, take handfuls of the potato-onion mixture and squeeze out as much liquid as possible. (You can also wrap the mixture in a kitchen towel and squeeze it out by twisting the ends of the towel, but I've always found it more effective and quicker to do it by hand.) Transfer the mixture to a large bowl, add the potato starch, sesame seeds, chile flakes, chile paste, and salt, and toss together. Add the beaten eggs and mix well. Transfer the mixture to a fine-mesh strainer set over the bowl so any excess liquid can drain.

In a large nonstick skillet, heat ¼ inch of oil over medium-high heat. Working in batches, put 2 rounded tablespoons of the mixture on a wide spatula and flatten it with your hand to form a 3-inch-wide pancake. Slide the pancake into the oil and cook until golden brown on the bottom, about 3 minutes. Flip and cook until the other side is golden brown and cooked through, 2 to 3 minutes more. Transfer to a wire rack or paper towel–lined plate to drain and season immediately with a little salt. Repeat with the remaining potato mixture, adding more oil to the skillet as needed. Serve the pancakes hot with the compote.

# KIMCHI PANCAKES
*KIMCHI JEON*

**MAKES ABOUT TWELVE 2½-INCH-WIDE PANCAKES**

There's something to be said for eating kimchi when it's young and fresh and still a little crisp. But when your kimchi gets really funky and fermented and you're scared of what it might do to your digestive system, that's the best time to make these pancakes. That's when the kimchi flavor really shines through. These pancakes are really tasty with their crispy outside and are so easy to make.

These are usually made as large pancakes that are cut into smaller pieces to be shared at the table, but I find smaller ones more attractive and easier to flip.

1 cup drained chopped Cabbage Kimchi (page 28), plus ¼ cup kimchi liquid

6 tablespoons rice flour

¼ cup all-purpose flour

3 tablespoons thinly sliced scallions

1 large egg

1 teaspoon sugar

½ teaspoon kosher salt or sea salt

Vegetable oil, for frying

Pancake Dipping Sauce (page 212), for serving

IN A MEDIUM BOWL, stir together the kimchi, kimchi liquid, rice flour, all-purpose flour, scallions, egg, sugar, and salt until a thick batter forms.

In a large nonstick skillet, heat 2 tablespoons of oil over medium heat. Working in batches, spoon 2 tablespoons of the batter into the skillet to form pancakes about 2½ inches wide. Cook until golden brown on the bottom, 3 to 4 minutes. Flip the pancakes and press down firmly on the pancakes with the back of your spatula. Continue cooking until the other side is golden brown, about 3 minutes more. Transfer to a wire rack or paper towel–lined plate to drain. Repeat with the remaining batter, adding more oil as needed.

Transfer to a platter and serve with the pancake dipping sauce.

# MUNG BEAN PANCAKES

*BINDAETTEOK*

**MAKES ABOUT FOURTEEN 3½-INCH-WIDE PANCAKES**

I have so many memories of my mom making these pancakes, and of eating them on the streets of Seoul. I fed these addictive, crispy pancakes to my head chef, Andy Hales, when we were exploring Gwangjang market together. We devoured them greedily, standing in the market alley, watching the chaos around us. No flour is used in these pancakes so they are great for those with gluten sensitivities; just be sure to use tamari, which is wheat-free, in lieu of soy sauce. Note that mung beans have a lengthy soaking time, so be sure to start early.

¾ cup mung bean sprouts, tails and any soft or brown pieces removed, rinsed, dried well, and chopped

½ cup drained finely chopped Cabbage Kimchi (page 28), plus ¼ cup kimchi liquid

4 ounces ground pork (about ½ cup)

3 scallions, cut on an angle into ½-inch pieces

3 cloves garlic, grated or minced

½ teaspoon soy sauce

½ teaspoon toasted sesame oil

½ teaspoon kosher salt or sea salt

¼ teaspoon grated peeled fresh ginger

Freshly ground black pepper

1 cup dried split mung beans, soaked in water at room temperature for 6 hours or up to a day and then drained

Vegetable oil, for frying

1 small fresh Korean red chile or Fresno chile, thinly sliced on an angle (optional)

Pancake Dipping Sauce (page 212), for serving

IN A LARGE BOWL, stir together the mung bean sprouts, kimchi, pork, scallions, garlic, soy sauce, sesame oil, salt, ginger, and pepper to taste. Set the pork mixture aside.

Rinse the drained soaked mung beans several times in cold water, and drain again. Transfer to a food processor or blender, add ½ cup water and the kimchi liquid, and blend until relatively smooth. Stir the pureed bean mixture into the pork mixture and mix well. The batter will be thick.

In a large nonstick skillet, heat 2 tablespoons of vegetable oil over medium heat. Working in batches, spoon ¼ cup of the batter into the skillet to form pancakes about 3½ inches wide. Sprinkle some chile slices (if using) onto the surface of the pancakes before they set. Cook, flipping halfway through, until both sides are browned and crisp, about 8 minutes total. Transfer to a wire rack or paper towel–lined plate to drain. Repeat with the remaining batter, adding more oil to the skillet as needed.

Transfer the pancakes to a platter and serve with the pancake dipping sauce.

# PANFRIED ZUCCHINI, MUSHROOM, AND TOFU

*HOBAK BUCHIM, BEOSEOT BUCHIM, DUBU BUCHIM*

**SERVES 4 TO 6**

These simple fried bites are quick, easy, and inexpensive to make. They're great as a snack for kids or to serve to friends as a nibble with beer.

½ cup all-purpose flour

3 large eggs, beaten

12 shiitake mushrooms, stemmed

7 ounces firm tofu, drained, cut into ½-inch slices, and dried between two layers of paper towels

1 small zucchini, cut into ½-inch slices

Kosher salt or sea salt

Freshly ground black pepper

Vegetable oil, for frying

1 fresh Korean red chile or Fresno chile, thinly sliced on an angle (optional)

Handful of fresh chives, cut into 1- to 2-inch pieces (optional)

Pancake Dipping Sauce (page 212), for serving

PUT THE FLOUR and beaten eggs into separate wide, shallow bowls. Spread the mushrooms, tofu, and zucchini out in a single layer on a baking sheet. Season lightly with salt and pepper and set aside for about 5 minutes so the seasonings soak in a bit. Lightly dredge the mushrooms, tofu, and zucchini in the flour, tapping off any excess.

In a large nonstick skillet, heat 2 tablespoons of oil over medium heat. Working in batches, coat the mushrooms in the eggs, letting any excess drip into the bowl, and place into the skillet. Cook, flipping halfway through, until golden, 6 to 8 minutes total. Transfer to a wire rack or paper towel–lined plate to drain. Repeat with the tofu and zucchini, adding more oil to the skillet as needed and, if desired, pressing the chile slices and chives onto their surfaces. Cook for about 3 minutes per side.

Transfer to a platter and serve immediately, with the dipping sauce.

# SEAFOOD PANCAKES

*HAEMUL PAJEON*

**MAKES THREE 7-INCH PANCAKES**

These pancakes are always a crowd-pleaser. They're chock-full of seafood and the crisp texture is addictive. My mom used to make them with squid and shrimp when guests came over. I've added scallops to make them extra special, but feel free to use whatever seafood you like. The pancakes are also a great way to use up any leftover vegetables you might have in the fridge. If you are using scallops, just make sure that they are very dry as any extra moisture will make for a soggy pancake.

¾ cup rice flour

6 tablespoons self-rising flour

2 tablespoons *doenjang* (Korean soybean paste)

½ teaspoon freshly ground black pepper

3 large pinches of kosher salt or sea salt

10 jumbo shrimp, peeled, deveined, halved lengthwise, and patted dry

4 large diver sea scallops, muscle removed, thinly sliced horizontally, and patted dry

5 scallions, julienned

2 large cloves garlic, grated or minced

2 fresh Korean red chiles or Fresno chiles, cut into long, thin strips

1 fresh Korean green chile or jalapeño, cut into long, thin strips

Vegetable oil, for frying

Pancake Dipping Sauce (page 212), for serving

IN A LARGE BOWL, gently whisk together the rice flour, self-rising flour, soybean paste, pepper, salt, and 1⅓ cups cold water until smooth. Add the shrimp, scallops, scallions, garlic, red chiles, and green chile and stir the batter until thoroughly combined.

In a large nonstick skillet, heat 3 tablespoons of oil over medium-high heat. Spoon in one-third of the batter and spread it evenly to form a pancake about 7 inches wide. Fry until golden brown and crispy on the bottom, 3 to 4 minutes. Carefully flip and cook until the other side is golden, 3 to 4 minutes more. Transfer to a paper towel–lined plate to drain. Repeat with the remaining batter, adding more oil to the skillet as needed.

Cut the pancakes into wedges and transfer to a serving platter. Serve immediately, with the dipping sauce.

# PANFRIED FISH

*SAENGSUN JEON*

**SERVES 4 TO 6**

In Korea, this is usually served as an appetizer or side dish, and it is one of my favorites. I have always loved seafood and I have even been known to eat this particular *jeon* cold! If you'd like to make it a main course, simply allow for one whole fillet per person. Cod is often the fish of choice for this dish, but since the fish needs to be sliced thinly, I like to use a variety that's already thin, like flounder or snapper. Really, any mild, white-fleshed fish will do, but if you do use a thick fish like cod, try partially freezing it to make it easier to slice.

⅓ cup all-purpose flour

1 large egg, beaten

3 boneless skinless flounder or
red snapper fillets (about 4 ounces each)

Kosher salt or sea salt

Freshly ground black pepper

Vegetable oil, for frying

1 small fresh Korean red chile or Fresno
chile, thinly sliced on an angle (optional)

Handful of fresh chives, cut into
1- to 2-inch pieces (optional)

Pancake Dipping Sauce (page 212),
for serving

PUT THE FLOUR and beaten egg into separate wide, shallow bowls. Cut each fish fillet crosswise at a slight angle into four or five pieces. Season lightly with salt and pepper and then set aside for about 5 minutes so the seasonings soak in a bit. Lightly dredge the fish in the flour, tapping off any excess.

In a large nonstick skillet, heat 2 tablespoons of oil over medium heat. Working in batches, coat the fish in the egg, letting any excess drip into the bowl, and place into the skillet. If desired, press a chile slice and some chives onto each piece in the skillet. Cook, flipping halfway through, until golden, about 4 minutes total. Transfer to a wire rack or paper towel–lined plate to drain. Repeat with the remaining fish, adding more oil to the skillet as needed.

Transfer the fish to a platter and serve immediately, with the dipping sauce.

# SEAFOOD FRITTERS

*HAEMUL BUCHIM*

**MAKES ABOUT TWENTY-EIGHT 2-INCH-WIDE FRITTERS**

These little fritters, cooked in just a touch of oil, feel a bit too easy to be such a hit at the table. They are surprisingly good! I have served these to adults and kids, and they always get swarmed. Any leftovers are also a cinch to pack in a lunch box. If I don't have shrimp at home, I simply do without and increase the amount of crab sticks.

**4 ounces crab sticks, cut into ½-inch pieces**

**12 large shrimp, peeled, deveined, halved lengthwise, and cut into ¼-inch pieces**

**2 scallions, whites thinly sliced and greens thickly sliced, both on an angle**

**3 large eggs**

**2½ tablespoons rice flour**

**Kosher salt or sea salt**

**Freshly ground black pepper**

**Vegetable oil, for frying**

**Pancake Dipping Sauce (page 212), for serving**

IN A MEDIUM BOWL, toss together the crab sticks, shrimp, and scallions. Add the eggs, break up the yolks, and give the mixture a good stir. Add the flour, season with salt and a generous amount of pepper, and mix well.

In a large nonstick skillet, heat 1 tablespoon of oil over medium heat. Working in batches, spoon about 1 tablespoon of the batter into the skillet to form fritters about 2 inches wide. (The seafood will poke out of the batter.) Cook, flipping halfway through, until lightly browned and cooked through, about 2 minutes total. Transfer to a platter, "chunky"-side up. Repeat with the remaining batter, adding more oil to the skillet as needed. Serve with the dipping sauce.

Pancakes, Dumplings, & Other Small Bites

# MEATY DUMPLINGS

## *MANDU*

**MAKES ABOUT 45 DUMPLINGS**

My mom used to enslave my sister and me to make these by the thousands. Plump dumplings neatly lined up on plates and trays covered every surface of the kitchen. I used to only eat the skins, shaking out the meaty insides for my sister. As I got older, I learned to savor those juicy gems as well, but the crispy skins are still my favorite part. If you prefer, the dumplings can be steamed instead of fried. These are a best seller at my restaurant, Jinjuu.

Filling:

**1 pound ground pork**

**½ pound ground beef**

**6 ounces firm tofu, drained and finely crumbled**

**2½ cups finely shredded Korean or napa cabbage leaves (ribs removed)**

**3 scallions, finely chopped**

**2½ tablespoons soy sauce**

**2 tablespoons toasted sesame oil**

**2 large cloves garlic, grated or minced**

**2 teaspoons kosher salt or sea salt**

**2 teaspoons grated peeled fresh ginger**

**2 teaspoons roasted sesame seeds**

**2 teaspoons sugar**

**¾ teaspoon freshly ground black pepper**

For the Dumplings:

**48 thin round eggless wonton wrappers**

**Vegetable oil, for frying**

**Dried chile threads (*silgochu*)**

**Chile-Soy Dipping Sauce (page 212), for serving**

FOR THE FILLING: In a large bowl, combine the filling ingredients. Mix together using your hands, really breaking up the tofu to yield a very uniform texture.

FOR THE DUMPLINGS: Line a couple of baking sheets with waxed paper and set aside. Fill a small bowl with water. Unwrap the wonton wrappers and cover lightly with a piece of plastic wrap to keep them from drying out. Lay a wrapper on a clean work surface and put a tablespoon of the meat filling in the center. Dip a forefinger into the water and run it along the edges of the wrapper to moisten the surface. Fold the wrapper in half. Starting at the top of the half-circle and working toward the ends, press firmly together to seal, pressing out any air bubbles.

Lay the dumpling on its side on one of the prepared baking sheets. Repeat with the remaining wrappers and filling, making sure the dumplings aren't touching on the baking sheets. Once the dumplings are assembled, if you don't plan to cook them right away, you can freeze them on the baking sheets, then bag them up to store in the freezer. Without thawing the frozen dumplings, boil or steam them to cook through, then pan fry if you like to make them crispy.

In a large nonstick skillet, heat about 1 tablespoon of vegetable oil over medium-high heat. Working in batches, lay the dumplings on their sides in the pan in a single layer without crowding the pan. Cook until golden brown on the bottom, 2 to 3 minutes. Flip them and cook until the other side is golden brown and the filling is cooked through, 2 to 3 minutes more. Transfer the fried dumplings to a wire rack or paper towel–lined plate to drain. Repeat with the remaining dumplings, adding more oil to the skillet as needed. If you prefer not to fry the dumplings, steam them in batches until cooked through, 5 to 6 minutes, then transfer to a serving platter (steamed dumplings do not need to be drained).

Transfer the fried dumplings to a platter. Top with some of the chile threads and serve immediately, with the dipping sauce.

TIP: *If you'd like to check the seasoning of the filling for the dumplings—or any kind of filling or stuffing that includes raw meat or fish—cook a small patty in a lightly oiled skillet, then adjust the seasonings to your taste.*

# KING DUMPLINGS

*WANG MANDU*

**MAKES 8 LARGE AND VERY PLUMP 4-INCH-WIDE DUMPLINGS**

These giant dumplings are originally from North Korea, and I have many memories of seeking them out in the back alleys of Insadong, Seoul. They can have either a taut, smooth skin or a fluffy, breadier kind used for steamed Chinese buns. It can be hard to find the extra-large wrappers needed for these large dumplings, so I've included the method for making them below. They're absolutely worth the effort.

You can steam the dumplings in a bamboo or metal steamer basket set over a wok, saucepan, or skillet or in a Western-style steamer set. Use two steamer baskets if you have them; otherwise, cook the dumplings in batches. If you prefer panfried dumplings, steam them as described and then fry them in some vegetable oil in a nonstick skillet until the skin is crispy.

Wrappers:

2¼ cups all-purpose flour,
plus more for dusting

1 large egg, beaten

1 teaspoon kosher salt or sea salt

1 teaspoon vegetable oil

½ cup hot water

Filling:

2 cloves garlic

1 (1-inch) knob fresh ginger, peeled

2 ounces shiitake mushrooms, stemmed and coarsely chopped

2 ounces sweet potato noodles (*dangmyun*), cooked according to package instructions, drained, and coarsely chopped

½ cup coarsely chopped Korean or napa cabbage leaves (ribs removed)

½ cup drained and chopped Cabbage Kimchi (page 29)

2 scallions, coarsely chopped

1 tablespoon soy sauce

1 tablespoon sugar

1 tablespoon toasted sesame oil

1 teaspoon crushed sesame seeds

1 teaspoon kosher salt or sea salt

¼ teaspoon freshly ground black pepper

3½ ounces firm tofu, drained and finely crumbled

¼ pound ground beef

¼ pound ground pork

2 large eggs, lightly beaten

Chile-Soy Dipping Sauce (page 212), for serving

**FOR THE WRAPPERS:** In a food processor, combine the flour, egg, salt, and oil and pulse a couple of times. With the motor running, slowly add the hot water until a tacky dough forms. Transfer to a clean work surface dusted with flour and knead lightly until smooth, 1 to 2 minutes. Cover with a damp cloth or plastic wrap and let rest at room temperature for at least 30 minutes and up to 1 hour.

**FOR THE FILLING:** Meanwhile, clean the food processor. With the motor running, drop in the garlic and ginger until finely chopped. Add the mushrooms, noodles, cabbage, kimchi, scallions, soy sauce, sugar, sesame oil, sesame seeds, salt, and pepper and process, scraping down the bowl once or twice, until finely chopped. Transfer to a large bowl, add the tofu, beef, pork, and beaten eggs, and gently mix using your hands until evenly incorporated. Cover and refrigerate until ready to assemble the dumplings.

Fill the base of your steamer setup with 1 inch of water. Cut 2 or 3 rounds of parchment paper just slightly smaller than the bottom of the steamer basket(s). Cut small holes in the parchment (similar to the way you made paper snowflakes as a kid) for the steam to go through. Set aside.

Divide the dough into 8 equal pieces and cover with plastic wrap or a damp towel as you work to keep them from drying out. On a clean work surface dusted with flour, roll one piece of dough into a round disc, rolling from the edge of the disc toward the middle and using less pressure as you get to the middle so that the center of the disc is slightly thicker than the edges. Rotate the disc and repeat the rolling and turning until the disc is about 6 inches wide. Transfer the wrapper to a baking sheet or platter lined with plastic wrap. Repeat with the remaining pieces of dough, sepa-rating the wrappers on the baking sheet with plastic wrap, if needed.

Fill a small bowl with water. Working with one wrapper at a time on a clean surface, spoon a scant ½ cup of the filling onto the center of the wrapper. Dip a forefinger in the water and run it along the edges of the wrapper to moisten the surface. Fold the wrapper in half away from you. Starting at the top of the half circle and working toward the ends, press firmly together to seal, pressing out any air bubbles.

Take the pointy ends of the half circle and pull them together, folding them downward and toward each other so they overlap slightly and form a shape that resembles a nurse's cap. Dab the place where the ends meet with a little water and pinch together to seal.

Lay the dumpling in the prepared steamer basket. Repeat with the remaining wrappers and filling, making sure to leave at least 1 inch of space between the dumplings, as they will expand when cooked. Cook the dumplings in batches, if needed.

Bring the water in the steamer base to a steady simmer. Set the steamer basket(s) over the water, cover, and steam the dumplings until cooked through, about 15 minutes. Repeat with the remaining dumplings, if needed. Serve immediately, with the dipping sauce.

---

**TIP:** *If you happen to have a tortilla press, you can use it to create a round disc from the dough at the beginning of the rolling process. The dough will shrink back a little when you remove it so you still need to roll it out, but the basic shape will be there.*

# LOTUS ROOT CHIPS

**MAKES ABOUT 5 CUPS**

Lotus root looks pretty homely when whole, but peel, thinly slice, and fry them up, and they transform into beautiful lacy (and tasty!) chips. I like to serve them with Krazy Korean Burgers (page 185), Spicy Tuna Tartare (page 73), and Steak Tartare (page 80). When purchasing lotus root, look for ones that are firm, smooth, and unbruised. And when cutting them for the chips, use a mandoline if you have one. At Jinjuu, we serve these delicate chips on top of *Bibimbap* (page 107) and Kimchi Fried Rice (page 115). I admit, I do snack on them on the pass!

**Vegetable oil, for frying**

**12 ounces fresh lotus root, peeled and cut into round slices no thicker than 1/16 inch (use a mandoline)**

**Kosher salt or sea salt**

***Gochugaru* (Korean chile flakes; optional)**

**IN A WIDE,** heavy-bottomed pot at least 5 inches deep, heat 2 inches of oil over medium-high heat until it reaches 375°F. Working in batches, slip the lotus root slices one by one into the oil. Fry, stirring occasionally, until the oil has stopped bubbling and the chips are golden brown, about 2 minutes. Transfer to a wire rack or paper towel–lined baking sheet to drain and immediately season with salt and chile flakes (if using). The chips will continue to darken and crisp up as they sit. Repeat with the remaining lotus root slices, letting the oil return to 375°F between batches. Serve warm or at room temperature.

**TIP:** *Don't use prepackaged peeled and sliced lotus root, which can be found in Asian markets, because they're way too thick and will usually have been treated with a preservative.*

# CANDIED SWEET POTATO WEDGES

## *GOGUMA MATTANG*

**SERVES 2**

If you've never had *mattang* before, your first bite will be a pleasant surprise: break through the crisp, light candy shell to reach the sweet, starchy potato, a wonderful combination. Use Korean sweet potatoes, which are sweeter and drier than American ones. They come in different sizes, but try to get potatoes that are slender and 3 to 4 inches long. They're perfect because all you need to do is quarter them.

Vegetable oil, for frying

1 pound Korean sweet potatoes, unpeeled, cut lengthwise into 1-inch-wide wedges

6 tablespoons sugar

2 teaspoons roasted sesame seeds

Flaky sea salt, such as Maldon

IN A LARGE, wide, heavy-bottomed pot, heat 3 inches of oil over medium-high heat until it reaches 375°F. Working in batches, if needed, fry the sweet potatoes until dark golden and crisp on the outside and just cooked through, 8 to 10 minutes. Transfer to a wire rack or paper towel–lined plate to drain. They will continue to cook after you remove them from the heat.

Meanwhile, in a large skillet, heat 1 tablespoon of oil over medium heat. Add the sugar and 2 tablespoons water and cook, stirring often, until the sugar melts and turns golden, about 5 minutes. Remove the skillet from the heat, add the fried potatoes, and carefully stir with tongs or chopsticks until they're evenly coated with the glaze.

Transfer the potatoes to a parchment paper–lined baking sheet, spreading them out so they don't touch one another. Thin threads of "candy" should form as you lift them out of the pan. Immediately sprinkle the potatoes with the sesame seeds and some salt. Let cool slightly so the candy shells set before serving.

TIP: *Use a stainless-steel skillet rather than a nonstick one when cooking the sugar because it's hard to see the sugar change color on a dark surface. To aid in the cleanup, add some hot water to the skillet right after emptying it out. It will soften any remaining candy.*

# DAD'S TOASTED RICE CAKES

## WITH SESAME OIL, GOCHUGARU, AND SALT

**SERVES 2**

My dad toasts rice cakes in the oven until they get nice and crusty on the outside and soft and chewy on the inside. He then drizzles them with sesame oil, chile flakes, and salt. So simple and satisfying. It's essential to use fresh—not frozen—cylindrical rice cakes for this recipe. The toothsome texture will prove to be addictive, and you'll soon find yourself craving these snacks.

½ pound (about ½ inch wide), fresh, long cylindrical rice cakes (*dduk*), cut into 3- to 3½-inch-long sticks and pulled apart

1 teaspoon vegetable oil

1 teaspoon toasted sesame oil

¼ teaspoon *gochugaru* (Korean chile flakes)

Generous pinch of kosher salt or sea salt

PREHEAT THE BROILER and position a rack 4 to 5 inches from the heat source.

Line a baking sheet with aluminum foil. Pile the rice cakes on the baking sheet, drizzle with the vegetable oil, and toss to coat. Arrange the rice cakes in single layer on the baking sheet. Broil until the outsides are lightly blistered and golden in spots and the insides are soft and heated through, about 4 minutes total, flipping halfway through. Be careful not to let them cook too long or the crust will get too hard.

Transfer to a platter and top with the sesame oil, chile flakes, and salt. Let the rice cakes cool slightly before serving.

TIP: *Instead of seasoning the rice cakes directly, you can mix some sesame oil, gochugaru, and salt in a small dish to serve alongside for dipping.*

# PAN-TOASTED RICE CAKES

*WITH HONEY AND SESAME SEEDS*

**SERVES 2**

Another way to toast rice cakes is in a skillet, where you have a little more control over how blistered and soft they get. I like to top these with another classic Korean combo: honey and sesame seeds.

2 teaspoons vegetable oil

½ pound (about ½ inch wide), fresh, long cylindrical rice cakes (*dduk*), cut into 3- to 3½-inch-long sticks and pulled apart

2 tablespoons honey

1 teaspoon toasted sesame oil

1 teaspoons roasted sesame seeds

Generous pinch of kosher salt or sea salt

IN A MEDIUM heavy-bottomed skillet, heat the vegetable oil over medium heat. Add the rice cakes, tossing to coat. The rice cakes will stick to one another initially; just separate them with tongs or chopsticks. Cook, shaking the pan occasionally, until the outsides are just barely golden in spots and the insides are warm and soft, about 10 minutes.

Transfer to a platter and top with the honey, sesame oil, sesame seeds, and salt. Let the rice cakes cool slightly before serving.

# SWEET BRAISED BLACK SOYBEANS

## *KONGJORIM*

**MAKES ABOUT 2 CUPS**

*Kongjorim* is another traditional *banchan*. These sweet-and-savory black soybeans, which cook up firmer than regular beans, are a nice respite for the palate. You'll want to make this tasty dish a regular on your Korean table.

**1 cup dried black soybeans, picked through, rinsed, and drained**

**3 tablespoons soy sauce**

**2 tablespoons brown sugar**

**2 tablespoons honey**

**2 tablespoons mirin**

**1 teaspoon toasted sesame oil**

**2 cloves garlic, grated or minced**

**1 tablespoon roasted sesame seeds**

IN A MEDIUM heavy-bottomed pot, combine the soybeans and enough water to cover by about 2 inches and bring to a boil over high heat, skimming off any foam that forms on the surface. Reduce the heat to maintain a simmer, uncovered, until firm but just starting to soften, about 1½ hours. If at any time the beans start to peek out from the water, add a cup of hot water.

Add the soy sauce, sugar, honey, mirin, sesame oil, and garlic and stir until the sugar has dissolved. Simmer, stirring occasionally, until the beans are still firm, but cooked, and the sauce is syrupy and glossy, about 1 hour. Remove from the heat and stir in the sesame seeds.

Transfer to a bowl or container and let cool to room temperature. These beans will keep, tightly covered, in the refrigerator for a couple of weeks.

Sweet Braised Black Soybeans

Crispy Anchovies (page 72)

# POTATO SALAD

*GAMJA SALAD*

**MAKES ABOUT 4 CUPS**

Korean potato salad is generally sweeter than its American counterpart and more closely resembles chunky mashed potatoes. Although it may seem out of place on the Korean table, it's a customary *banchan*.

1 pound Yukon Gold potatoes, peeled and cut into 1-inch pieces

Kosher salt or sea salt

1 large carrot, julienned

¼ cup frozen corn kernels

2 large eggs, hard-boiled, peeled, and diced

1 Honeycrisp or other crisp apple, cored and diced

½ cup mayonnaise, preferably Kewpie or a Korean brand

2 tablespoons finely chopped fresh chives, plus more for serving

4½ teaspoons rice vinegar

1 teaspoon sugar

Freshly ground black pepper

PUT THE POTATOES in a medium saucepan, add cold water to cover by 1 inch, and salt the water generously. Bring to a boil over high heat, then reduce the heat to maintain a simmer until tender, 15 to 20 minutes. Use a slotted spoon to transfer the potatoes to a colander to drain. Return the saucepan of water to a boil. Meanwhile, transfer the drained potatoes to a large bowl and lightly smash with a fork or potato masher. Let the smashed potatoes cool.

Add the carrot and corn to the boiling water and cook until the carrot is tender, about 1 minute. Drain, rinse under cold water, then drain again. Add the carrot and corn to the smashed potatoes and then add the eggs and apple.

In a small bowl, stir together the mayonnaise, chives, vinegar, and sugar. Add the mayo mixture to the potato mixture, season with salt and pepper, and toss to coat. Garnish with chives, and refrigerate until cold before serving.

# SEASONED SPINACH

*SHIGEUMCHI NAMUL*

**SERVES 4**

Flavored with sesame, soy sauce, vinegar, and sugar, this is another classic *banchan*. Mature spinach, with its contrasting textures of sturdy stems and velvety leaves, is a better choice than baby spinach here.

Kosher salt or sea salt

2 tablespoons toasted sesame oil

1 tablespoon soy sauce

1 teaspoon crushed roasted sesame seeds

1 teaspoon rice vinegar

1 teaspoon sugar

2 cloves garlic, grated or minced

Freshly ground black pepper

1 pound spinach, stem ends trimmed

BRING A LARGE POT of salted water to a boil and prepare an ice water bath. Meanwhile, in a medium bowl, combine the sesame oil, soy sauce, sesame seeds, vinegar, sugar, garlic, and pepper to taste and stir until the sugar has dissolved. Set the sesame dressing aside.

Blanch the spinach in the boiling water until just wilted and then shock in the ice water bath. Drain well and squeeze out any excess water. Gently loosen the clumps of spinach with your fingers, transfer to the bowl of sesame dressing, and toss together. Cover and refrigerate for about 1 hour to let the flavors meld before serving.

Seasoned Soybean Sprouts

Seasoned Spinach (page 67)

# SEASONED SOYBEAN SPROUTS

*KONG NAMUL*

**MAKES ABOUT 3 CUPS**

Seasoned soybean sprouts are one of the classic non-spicy *banchan* to grace the table. Soybean sprouts have a larger, more vibrant yellow head and a fatter body than the more readily available mung bean sprouts. Even after cooking, the heads remain crunchy and add a nice contrast to the lightly wilted roots. It was my job when I was younger to pinch the strandlike tails off—it was a chore, but well worth the effort. Soybean sprouts can be found in plastic bags in Asian markets. They are highly perishable, so be sure to use them within a day or two.

**3 cups soybean sprouts**

**Kosher salt or sea salt**

**1 scallion, green part only, thinly sliced on an angle**

**1 clove garlic, grated or minced**

**1 tablespoon roasted sesame seeds**

**1 tablespoon toasted sesame oil**

PINCH THE SCRAGGLY TAILS and any brown spots off of the sprouts. Rinse well, discarding any loose husks. In a small saucepan, combine the sprouts, ½ cup water, and a generous pinch of salt. Cover, bring to a boil over high heat, and boil for about 10 minutes. Drain, rinse under cold water until cool, and drain again. Gently squeeze out any excess water.

In a medium bowl, stir together the scallion, garlic, sesame seeds, and sesame oil. Add the bean sprouts, season with salt, and gently toss to coat.

# EGG CUSTARDS WITH SHRIMP

*SAEWOO GYERANJJIM*

**SERVES 4**

These silky, light, and super-easy egg custards are good on their own and even better topped with sweet shrimp and sliced scallions. Take care not to overcook these, as the texture can become tough and dry. Even though *gyeranjjim* is usually served as a *banchan*, for a simple meal, serve them with Watercress Salad (page 89) and brown rice.

8 large eggs

2 cups chicken stock

2 teaspoons fish sauce

½ teaspoon kosher salt or sea salt

8 small shrimp, peeled and deveined

1 scallion, thinly sliced on an angle

Toasted sesame oil, for serving

Roasted sesame seeds, for serving

BRING A POT of water to a boil. In a large bowl, whisk together the eggs, stock, fish sauce, and salt. Pour the mixture into four 10-ounce heatproof bowls or ramekins. Arrange the bowls in a large wide pot with a lid. Add enough boiling water to the pot to reach two-thirds of the way up the sides of the bowls. Bring the water to a gentle simmer, cover the pot, and steam until the custards are slightly wobbly in the center, 6 to 7 minutes.

Divide the shrimp and scallion among the bowls, cover, and steam until the shrimp are cooked through and the custards are set, about 3 minutes more. Top the custards with a drizzle of sesame oil and a sprinkle of sesame seeds and serve warm.

# CRISPY ANCHOVIES

*MYULCHI BOKKEUM*

**MAKES ABOUT ¾ CUP**

Dried anchovies can be found in all different sizes in Korean markets. The largest ones are used to make stock. The tiniest ones are used in this dish, although you can use the second smallest ones as well. This is a common addition to lunch boxes, and I have many memories of snacking on these. Kids love the saltiness, sweetness, and stickiness of this *banchan*.

1 cup tiny dried anchovies (*jan-myulchi*), rinsed and drained

1 tablespoon vegetable oil

2 cloves garlic, grated or minced

1 tablespoon mirin

4½ teaspoons honey

1 teaspoon soy sauce

1½ teaspoons roasted sesame seeds

1 teaspoon toasted sesame oil

1 fresh Korean green chile, twist pepper, or jalapeño, thinly sliced (optional)

1 scallion, thinly sliced on an angle

HEAT A LARGE SKILLET over medium heat, add the anchovies, and cook, stirring often, until any moisture has evaporated, about 5 minutes. Add the vegetable oil and cook, stirring often, until the anchovies are light golden, about 5 minutes more. Transfer to a small bowl.

In the same skillet, combine the garlic, mirin, honey, soy sauce, and 1 tablespoon water and bring to a boil over high heat. Reduce the heat to maintain a simmer until the sauce thickens, 1 to 2 minutes. Add the anchovies, stir to coat, and cook, stirring, until the anchovies are well glazed, about 1 minute more. Remove from the heat and stir in the sesame seeds, sesame oil, chile (if using), and scallion. Transfer to a bowl and serve.

# SPICY TUNA TARTARE

**SERVES 2**

This isn't the spicy tuna you find in most sushi joints. Instead of using the ubiquitous Sriracha-mayo combo, I season the tartare with my Spicy Korean Mustard Vinaigrette (page 217). The result is lighter and more vibrant and clean tasting. It also goes very well with Lotus Root Chips (page 58); you can either spoon a little on the delicate chips or serve the chips on the side. As always, when consuming raw fish, make sure it's fresh and of the highest quality.

8 ounces sashimi-quality tuna, diced into ¼-inch cubes

Heaping ⅓ cup finely diced seedless cucumber

2 tablespoons thinly sliced scallions or fresh chives

2 tablespoons finely chopped shallots

2 tablespoons Spicy Korean Mustard Vinaigrette (page 217)

4 teaspoons toasted sesame oil

2 teaspoons roasted sesame seeds, plus more for serving

2 teaspoons black sesame seeds, plus more for serving

2 perilla leaves (*ggaennip*), also known as sesame leaves, chopped, plus 1 leaf, julienned, for serving

Pinch of kosher salt or sea salt

IN A MEDIUM BOWL, gently toss together all the ingredients. Divide the tartare between two bowls or plates and sprinkle with additional roasted and black sesame seeds and the julienned perilla leaf. Serve immediately.

TIP: *Add more Spicy Korean Mustard Vinaigrette, if you like. And feel free to increase the amount of mustard too, if you like a bit more kick.*

# "BUFFALO" WINGS

**MAKES 24 TO 26 PIECES**

This is my version of Buffalo wings, tossed in a Korean-style hot sauce. If you can't find precut "party wings," get regular wings, cut off and discard the tips, and separate the wings at the main joint. Wings can vary quite a bit in size, but 3 pounds of average wings will give you a total of 24 to 26 drumettes and wingettes.

Sauce:

½ cup (1 stick) unsalted butter

6 tablespoons Korean apple vinegar (*sagwa-shikcho*) or rice vinegar

6 tablespoons *gochujang* (Korean chile paste)

1 teaspoon *gochugaru* (Korean chile flakes)

Chicken:

2 teaspoons garlic powder

2 teaspoons onion powder

2 teaspoons kosher salt or sea salt

1 teaspoon baking powder

½ teaspoon freshly ground black pepper

3 pounds chicken drumettes and wingettes or flats (also called "party wings")

¾ cup potato starch

Vegetable oil, for frying

FOR THE SAUCE: In a small saucepan, melt the butter over medium heat. Whisk in the vinegar, chile paste, and chile flakes until smooth and set aside in a warm spot.

FOR THE CHICKEN: In a small bowl, stir together the garlic powder, onion powder, salt, baking powder, and pepper. Put the chicken in a large bowl, sprinkle with the garlic powder mixture, and toss to coat. Let sit for 5 to 10 minutes. Sprinkle the potato starch over the chicken and toss again, making sure the chicken is well coated.

In a large, wide, heavy-bottomed pot at least 5 inches deep, heat 2 inches of oil over medium-high heat until it reaches 375°F. Working in batches, fry the chicken, stirring occasionally, until golden brown and cooked through, 8 to 10 minutes total. Transfer to a wire rack or paper towel–lined plate to drain. Let the oil return to 375°F between batches.

Put the cooked wings in a very large bowl. If the sauce has separated, give it a good whisk to bring it back together. Drizzle it over the chicken and toss until well coated. Serve immediately.

# LOTUS ROOT AND BEEF PATTIES

*YEONGEUN WANJA JEON*

**MAKES ABOUT 18 PATTIES,
DEPENDING ON THE DIAMETER OF THE LOTUS ROOT**

Lotus root adds a pretty, lacy cap to these otherwise modest-looking patties, as well as a slightly crisp, starchy accent. To keep the patties at one or two bites each, I like to use small lotus root. Larger ones will work fine, too, but will result in fewer patties since you'll need more meat per lotus root slice. These look very impressive when they come to the table. Be prepared for applause!

Kosher salt or sea salt

18 (⅛-inch-thick) slices small peeled lotus root (about 5 ounces and 2 inches wide)

Freshly ground black pepper

½ pound ground beef

3½ ounces firm tofu, drained and finely crumbled

¼ cup finely chopped onion

1 scallion, thinly sliced on an angle

2 large cloves garlic, grated or minced

1½ teaspoons sugar

2 teaspoons toasted sesame oil

1 teaspoon crushed roasted sesame seeds

1 teaspoon soy sauce

⅓ cup all-purpose flour or rice flour

2 large eggs, lightly beaten

Vegetable oil, for frying

18 perilla leaves (*ggaennip*), also known as sesame leaves, for serving (optional)

Pancake Dipping Sauce (page 212), for serving

BRING A SMALL saucepan of salted water to a boil. Blanch the lotus roots until crisp-tender, about 5 minutes. Drain, rinse under cold water to cool, drain again, and pat dry. Season lightly with salt and pepper and set aside.

In a large bowl, combine the beef, tofu, onion, scallion, garlic, sugar, sesame oil, sesame seeds, soy sauce, 1 teaspoon salt, and ¼ teaspoon pepper and gently mix using your hands, being careful not to overmix. Shape the beef mixture into ½-inch-thick rounds the same diameter as the lotus root. Press a lotus root slice onto each patty.

Put the flour and eggs into separate wide, shallow bowls. Lightly dredge the patties in the flour, tapping off any excess. In a large nonstick skillet, heat 2 tablespoons of oil over medium heat. Working in batches, coat the patties in the eggs, letting any excess drip into the bowl. Immediately put the patties in the skillet, lotus root–side up. Cook, flipping halfway through, until lightly browned, 6 to 8 minutes total. Transfer to a wire rack or paper towel–lined plate to drain. Repeat with the remaining patties, adding more oil to the skillet as needed.

Transfer the patties to a platter and serve immediately, with perilla leaves for wrapping around the patties, if desired, and the dipping sauce.

# SOY-BRAISED BEEF STRIPS AND QUAIL EGGS

## *JANGJORIM*

**SERVES 4 TO 6**

This is a somewhat salty side dish meant to be eaten in small amounts with rice and other dishes. While quail eggs are the classic accompaniment, feel free to substitute four chicken eggs. Hard-boil them separately, peel, and add to the pot after shredding the meat, making sure to submerge them in the salty broth so they absorb the flavor.

1 pound beef skirt steak, cut crosswise into 2-inch-wide pieces

1 onion, quartered

1 leek, white part only, thickly sliced

4 ounces Korean white radish (*mu*) or daikon, peeled and coarsely chopped

10 cloves garlic

1 (4-inch-long) piece dried kelp (*dashima*)

1 teaspoon whole black peppercorns

4 ounces small Korean twist peppers (*gwari gochu*), *shishito*, or Padrón peppers

¾ cup soy sauce

¾ cup sugar

Freshly ground black pepper

8 quail eggs, washed well

Black sesame seeds, for serving (optional)

IN A LARGE heavy-bottomed pot, combine the beef, onion, leek, radish, 2 cloves of the garlic, the kelp, peppercorns, and 8 cups cold water and bring to a boil over high heat. Reduce the heat to maintain a simmer, skimming off any fat and scum, until the meat is fork-tender, 1 to 1½ hours.

Transfer the beef to a large saucepan. Pass the braising liquid through a fine-mesh strainer into a large bowl and discard the solids. Pour 2 cups of the liquid over the beef, reserving the rest for another use. Add the peppers, soy sauce, sugar, remaining 8 cloves garlic, and black pepper to taste. Gently nestle in the quail eggs. Simmer for about 8 minutes and then remove the eggs. Unpeel one to make sure it's cooked through. If it is, transfer all the eggs to a bowl of cold water; once cool, peel them and set aside. If it's not, cook a minute or two longer. Meanwhile, simmer the meat mixture for 15 minutes more.

Remove the saucepan from the heat and transfer the meat to a cutting board. Coarsely shred or slice the meat with the grain (in the same direction as the grain). Return the meat and peeled eggs to the saucepan, submerging them in the broth, and let cool. Serve at room temperature, sprinkled with sesame seeds, if you like, or transfer to a container, cover, and refrigerate, then serve cold.

# CHILE BOMBS

## *GOCHU BOMBS*

**MAKES 24**

I like to stuff Korean twist peppers with a shortcut version of the meat mixture from my Krazy Korean Burgers (page 185). It's a little time intensive to assemble the stuffed peppers, but they fry up quickly and are worth the effort. This is a bit of a cross between an American jalapeño popper and a dumpling. At Jinjuu, we serve a variation of these with a great cool ranch dressing to dampen the heat.

Twist peppers come in all different sizes, and as the name suggests, they're often curled up and twisted rather than straight. For ease of stuffing these peppers, pick out larger, straighter ones. We can't source twist peppers for my restaurant in London, so we use jalapeños instead, which are a more than acceptable substitute.

**3 ounces ground beef (about ½ cup)**

**1 ounce pancetta, finely chopped (about ¼ cup)**

**1 small clove garlic, grated or minced**

**½ teaspoon onion powder**

**½ teaspoon *doenjang* (Korean soybean paste)**

**½ teaspoon *gochujang* (Korean chile paste)**

**¼ teaspoon *gochugaru* (Korean chile flakes)**

**¼ teaspoon sugar**

**¼ teaspoon roasted sesame seeds**

**24 large, relatively straight Korean twist peppers (*gwari gochu*) or medium jalapeños**

**1 ounce Monterey Jack cheese, cut into 24 sticks thin enough to easily fit into the peppers**

**½ cup all-purpose flour**

**2 large eggs, lightly beaten**

**1½ cups panko bread crumbs**

**Vegetable oil, for frying**

**Korean Ketchup (page 216) and/or Doenjang Mayonnaise (page 216), for serving**

IN A MEDIUM BOWL, combine the beef, pancetta, garlic, onion powder, soybean paste, chile paste, chile flakes, sugar, and sesame seeds and use your hands to mix well. Set aside.

Using a paring knife, cut a small slit lengthwise along one side of each pepper. Next, cut a small slit crosswise along the top to form a "T", leaving the stems attached. Remove the seeds from this opening, using the tip of the paring knife or a very small spoon to scrape them out. Be gentle, as the peppers have thin walls that can split easily. (It's not absolutely necessary to remove the seeds, but it will leave more space for the filling.)

Put a stick of cheese inside each pepper and then stuff with as much of the meat mixture as possible. It may help to use the tip of the paring knife to help push both the cheese and meat mixture in. Press the cut edges of the pepper together to close it a bit, smoothing any protruding meat mixture.

Put the flour, beaten eggs, and panko in three separate wide, shallow bowls. Working in batches, dredge the peppers in the flour and tap off any excess. Don't be afraid to get flour into the grooves of the peppers, as that will give the egg something to cling to. Coat the peppers in the eggs, letting any excess to drip into the bowl. (If you have a small silicone brush, I find it easier to put the peppers in the bowl and brush them lightly with the eggs.) Last, press the peppers into the panko to coat. Set them on a platter and repeat with the remaining peppers.

In a large, wide, heavy-bottomed pot at least 5 inches deep, heat 2 inches of oil over medium-high heat until it reaches 375°F. Working in batches, suspend each pepper in the oil for a couple of seconds to set the crust before letting it slip completely into the oil (otherwise, it will stick to the bottom of the pot). Fry, stirring occasionally, until golden, 1 to 1½ minutes. Transfer to a wire rack or paper towel–lined plate to drain. Repeat with the remaining peppers, letting the oil return to 375°F between batches.

Once the peppers have cooled slightly, transfer to a platter and serve with Korean ketchup and/or Doenjang Mayonnaise.

# STEAK TARTARE

## *YUKHWE*

**SERVES 4**

Korean steak tartare differs from Western versions in that the beef is flavored with sesame oil, pine nuts, and Asian pear, which lends crispness, sweetness, and freshness. I think you'll be pleasantly surprised. The beef is also usually cut into ribbons, but I like to dice mine. As with any meat that is to be served raw, use the best quality and freshest available.

1 small Asian pear or other firm but ripe pear, peeled, cored, and julienned

3 tablespoons fresh lemon juice

10 ounces filet mignon (preferably prime), trimmed and diced

2 tablespoons thinly sliced scallions (sliced on an angle)

1 tablespoon toasted sesame oil

1 tablespoon finely chopped shallots

1 tablespoon pine nuts, toasted

1 teaspoon finely grated lemon zest

Kosher salt or sea salt

Freshly ground black pepper

For Serving:

4 quail egg yolks (optional)

Scallions, thinly sliced on an angle

Handful of pine nuts, toasted

Dried chile threads (*silgochu*)

Lotus Root Chips (page 58; optional)

PUT THE PEAR in a small bowl of cold water with 1 tablespoon of the lemon juice to prevent it from turning brown. Let sit for 5 to 10 minutes and then drain well.

In a medium bowl, toss together the beef, remaining 2 tablespoons lemon juice, scallions, sesame oil, shallots, pine nuts, lemon zest, and salt and pepper to taste. Gently stir ½ cup of the julienned pears into the tartare.

To serve, mound the tartare in the center of four plates. If desired, make a small well in each mound of beef and put an egg yolk in each. Top with the remaining pear and garnish with scallions, pine nuts, and chile threads. Serve immediately, with lotus root chips, if desired.

TIP: *If not serving the tartare immediately, feel free to serve with lemon wedges on the side instead of mixing in the juice. This will help keep the beef's red color intact as the lemon juice will "cook" the meat slightly.*

# BLOOD SAUSAGE WRAPPED IN A BLANKET

### MAKES SIXTEEN 2½-INCH PIECES

This is my take on everyone's favorite party hors d'oeuvres, pigs in a blanket. Instead of mini hot dogs, I use Korean blood sausage (*soondae*), which is mildly spiced and includes glutinous rice, sweet potato noodles, scallions, and garlic. People generally purchase it steamed and sliced at food stalls in Korean markets, where it comes with a small container of salt, pepper, *gochugaru*, and sesame seeds for dipping. You can also buy packages of it in the refrigerated section at Korean markets like H-Mart and steam it at home, as well as make your own seasoning mix (see Tip, below).

Fresh blood sausage doesn't reheat very well, so just make sure you use it soon after buying or steaming it. It can be at room temperature when you wrap it in the pastry.

---

**Flour, for dusting**

**1 (14-ounce) sheet puff pastry, thawed**

**About 12 ounces steamed Korean blood sausage (*soondae*), cut on an angle into 16 slices, not including any end pieces**

**1 large egg yolk, lightly beaten with a splash of water**

**Dipping salt that comes with the sausage**

**Toasted sesame seeds (optional)**

**¼ cup prepared Korean mustard (*gyeoja*) or English mustard, for serving (optional)**

PREHEAT THE OVEN to 375°F. Line a baking sheet with parchment paper or a silicone baking mat.

On a lightly floured surface, roll the pastry into a 10 x 15-inch rectangle, then cut it into sixteen 2½-inch squares. Arrange a slice of sausage diagonally across one square of pastry. Dab some of the egg mixture on one corner, then lift it over the sausage to join the opposite corner; pinch and then twist together at the tips, wrapping the sausage with the pastry. Transfer to the prepared baking sheet.

Repeat with the remaining pastry and sausage. Brush the tops of the pastries with the remaining egg mixture and sprinkle with some dipping salt and sesame seeds (if using). Bake for 20 to 25 minutes, until the pastry is golden, rotating the baking sheet halfway through. Serve warm, with the remaining dipping salt and mustard, if desired.

---

TIP: *You can make your own dipping salt by mixing together 2 tablespoons kosher salt or sea salt, ¼ teaspoon freshly ground black pepper, ¼ teaspoon sesame seeds, and ⅛ teaspoon gochugaru.*

TIP: *Store-bought prepared Korean mustard, found in small tubes, can vary in spiciness. For more control, make your own prepared Korean mustard from its powdered form (gyeojagaru): Mix Korean (or English) mustard powder with an equal amount of water to form a thick paste. Cover and set aside in a warm spot for about 10 minutes to let the flavors develop.*

# KIMCHI PULLED PORK DISCO FRIES

**SERVES 4 TO 6**

Disco fries—slathered with gravy and melted cheese—are a classic diner staple in my home state of New Jersey. Here's my Korean American version.

1 pound frozen shoestring French fries

¾ teaspoon cornstarch

¾ cup chicken stock

1 tablespoon vegetable oil

1 cup Korean Pulled Pork (page 202)

Kosher salt or sea salt

¾ cup grated sharp cheddar or Gruyère cheese

¾ cup drained Cabbage Kimchi (page 28), finely chopped

½ cup sour cream

1 tablespoon Sriracha sauce

¼ cup chopped red onion

8 to 10 slices pickled jalapeños, drained

Handful of chopped fresh chives, for serving (optional)

COOK THE FRENCH FRIES according to the package instructions. Meanwhile, in a small bowl, whisk the cornstarch into the stock and then set the slurry aside. In a medium nonstick skillet, heat the oil over medium-high heat. Add the pork and cook, stirring occasionally, until heated through, about 3 minutes. Stir the slurry into the pork and cook, stirring, until the mixture thickens, about 2 minutes, and then keep warm.

When the fries are almost ready, preheat the broiler and position a rack 4 to 5 inches from the heat source.

Transfer the fries to a large shallow baking dish or broiler-safe platter and season with salt. Sprinkle the cheese on top and broil until the cheese melts, about 1 minute. Spread the pork mixture on top, followed by the kimchi. Spoon small dollops of the sour cream all over, drizzle with the Sriracha, and top with the onion, jalapeños, and chives, if using. Eat the disco fries before they get all soggy.

# SALADS & VEGGIES

# WATERCRESS SALAD

*MINARI MUCHIM*

**SERVES 4**

My mom used to make this very often and I'd eat it simply with rice and kimchi. This is usually made with Minari (Korean water dropwort) or water parsley but it is difficult to locate, so I find that watercress makes a good substitute. I like to serve this salad with my Egg Custards with Shrimp (page 70) and a bowl of brown rice for a simple meal. Or make a smaller batch and serve as a *banchan*. Watercress's nice peppery and spicy bite cuts through much of Korea's rich food. It's a wonderful palate cleanser. My only complaint about the green is that it's so perishable. If you buy it by the bunch, which is how it's commonly found in Asian markets, store it upside-down in ice or icy water. However, I find that bagged watercress holds up longer in the fridge and is a lot more convenient.

Juice of ½ lemon

1 tablespoon mirin

1 tablespoon toasted sesame oil

2 teaspoons soy sauce

1 small clove garlic, grated or minced

⅛ teaspoon kosher salt or sea salt

Generous pinch of *gochugaru* (Korean chile flakes)

4 ounces watercress (or *minari*), large stems removed

IN A LARGE BOWL, stir together the lemon juice, mirin, sesame oil, soy sauce, garlic, salt, and chile flakes. Add the watercress and toss to coat. Serve immediately.

# SPICY SCALLION AND RED ONION SALAD

## PA MUCHIM

### SERVES 6

I like this sharp and spicy salad with barbecued meats and lettuce wraps (page 188), as it helps cut through the richness of the meat and sauces. Wait until just before serving to drain and dress the scallions so they stay crisp. It is also a brilliant accompaniment to steamed fish.

8 scallions, cut into very thin 5-inch-long strips

½ small red onion, thinly sliced

2 tablespoons soy sauce

3½ tablespoons Korean apple vinegar (*sagwa-shikcho*) or rice vinegar

1 tablespoon toasted sesame oil

2 teaspoons *gochugaru* (Korean chile flakes)

2 tablespoons sugar

Kosher salt or sea salt

PUT THE SCALLIONS and onion in a large bowl of ice water and soak until the scallions curl up, at least 5 minutes or up to 2 hours in the refrigerator.

When ready to serve, drain well, spin in a salad spinner or pat dry. In a medium bowl, whisk the soy sauce, vinegar, sesame oil, chile flakes, sugar, and a pinch of salt until the sugar dissolves. Add the scallions and red onion and toss to coat.

TIP: *There is a Japanese tool called a negi cutter (negi is Japanese for "scallion") that I use to shred scallions. It looks like a paint brush handle, but there are several blades attached in lieu of bristles. Just run the blades along a length of scallion to easily and quickly shred it.*

# KIMCHI-APPLE SLAW

### SERVES 4

I like to serve this slaw with any of my barbecued meats, but it pairs especially well with Grilled Hanger Steak (page 190) and Roasted Pork Belly Lettuce Wraps (page 200).

¼ cup mayonnaise, preferably Kewpie or a Korean brand

2 teaspoons Korean apple vinegar (*sagwa-shikcho*) or rice vinegar

1 teaspoon sugar

½ teaspoon prepared Korean mustard (*gyeoja*) or English mustard

1 small Granny Smith apple, peeled, cored, and julienned

1 small cucumber, seeded and julienned

½ cup thinly sliced Cabbage Kimchi (page 28) with liquid

Kosher salt or sea salt

IN A MEDIUM BOWL, stir together the mayonnaise, vinegar, sugar, and mustard. Add the apple, cucumber, and kimchi and toss with the dressing. Season with salt and refrigerate until cold before serving.

# SOY-GLAZED TOFU SALAD

*DUBU BUCHIM*

**SERVES 4**

This vegetarian recipe is a healthy yet satisfying salad that I often make as an appetizer. The vibrant flavors of the glaze and the fragrant mix of leaves in the salad are a wonderful combination. I even like to just make the tofu to serve on its own—the dressing, with its slight spice and hint of honey, wins over your guests every time.

14 ounces firm or extra-firm tofu, drained and sliced crosswise into 8 or 12 rectangles

2 tablespoons mirin

1 tablespoon *gochujang* (Korean chile paste)

1 tablespoon honey

1 tablespoon soy sauce

2 teaspoons toasted sesame oil

2 scallions, thinly sliced on an angle

1 clove garlic, grated or minced

1 teaspoon roasted sesame seeds

1 tablespoon vegetable oil

Kosher salt or sea salt

6 cups mixed greens, such as baby spinach and frisée

3 or 4 perilla leaves (*ggaennip*), also known as sesame leaves, torn into bite-size pieces (optional)

1 fresh Korean red chile or Fresno chile, thinly sliced on an angle, for serving

SPREAD OUT THE TOFU slices on a paper towel–lined plate, press another layer of paper towels on top, and let sit for 5 to 10 minutes to dry. Meanwhile, in a small bowl, stir together the mirin, chile paste, honey, soy sauce, and sesame oil until smooth. Stir in the scallions, garlic, and sesame seeds and set the dressing aside.

In a large nonstick skillet, heat the vegetable oil over medium heat. Working in batches, if needed, gently slide the tofu into the skillet and fry until golden brown, 4 to 5 minutes per side. Lightly season with salt.

In a large bowl, combine the greens and perilla leaves (if using) and toss with 2 tablespoons of the dressing. Divide the salad among four plates and top each with 2 or 3 slices of tofu. Spoon additional dressing over the tofu and garnish with the chile. Serve immediately.

# BROCCOLI, MUSHROOM, AND SESAME SALAD

**SERVES 4 TO 6**

This light fresh salad can be served as a *banchan* or as a larger plate. You'll find that it is quite tasty, and the nuttiness of the sesame oil paired with the tartness of the apple vinegar is a great combination.

**Kosher salt or sea salt**

**2 tablespoons roasted sesame seeds**

**1 tablespoon toasted sesame oil**

**1 tablespoon soy sauce**

**1 tablespoon Korean apple vinegar (*sagwa-shikcho*) or rice vinegar**

**¼ teaspoon *gochugaru* (Korean chile flakes), plus more for garnish (optional)**

**2 cloves garlic, grated or minced**

**5 cups broccoli florets (about 6 ounces)**

**4 ounces button mushrooms, stems trimmed and thinly sliced**

**2 scallions, thinly sliced on an angle**

BRING A LARGE POT of salted water to a boil and prepare an ice water bath. Meanwhile, in a large bowl, stir together the sesame seeds, sesame oil, soy sauce, vinegar, chile flakes, garlic, and salt to taste. Set the dressing aside.

Blanch the broccoli in the boiling water until crisp-tender, 1½ to 2 minutes, and then shock in the ice water bath. Drain well. Add the blanched broccoli, mushrooms, and scallions to the bowl with the dressing and toss to coat. Transfer to a platter, sprinkle with chile flakes, if desired, and serve.

# SUPERFOODS SALAD
## *WITH CARROT-GINGER DOENJANG DRESSING*

**SERVES 4 TO 6**

Chock-full of superfoods like avocado, kale, sunflower seeds, and ginger, this salad is worth adding to your mealtime repertoire and takes no time to throw together. I like to make extra dressing and use it as a healthy dip for crudités or as a spread on sandwiches. It will keep in the fridge for up to a week.

Dressing:

1 carrot, coarsely chopped

¾-inch knob fresh ginger, peeled and coarsely chopped

2 tablespoons vegetable oil

2 tablespoons rice vinegar

1 tablespoon *doenjang* (Korean soybean paste)

1 tablespoon fresh lemon juice

1½ teaspoons mirin

1½ teaspoons toasted sesame oil

Kosher salt or sea salt

Freshly ground black pepper

Salad:

6 ounces kale, stemmed and coarsely chopped

1 red bell pepper, finely chopped

1 small carrot, shaved into ribbons with a peeler or mandoline

½ red onion, finely chopped, soaked in cold water for 10 minutes, and drained well

¼ cup hulled toasted sunflower seeds

1 firm but ripe avocado, halved, pitted, and peeled

½ lime (optional)

FOR THE DRESSING: In a blender, combine all the dressing ingredients with salt and pepper to taste and process until smooth. Pour the dressing into a small bowl and set aside.

FOR THE SALAD: In a large bowl of cold water, massage the kale vigorously for about 3 minutes to break down the chewy fibers. Drain, dry well, and transfer to a large bowl. Add the bell pepper, carrot, onion, and sunflower seeds and toss together. Drizzle ¼ cup of the dressing over the salad and toss to coat, adding more to taste.

Divide the salad among four to six plates. Cut the avocado into thin wedges and squeeze some lime juice over top, if desired. Arrange the avocado on the salads and serve immediately.

# FRISÉE, PERSIMMON, POMEGRANATE, AND FETA SALAD

*WITH SPICY KOREAN MUSTARD VINAIGRETTE*

**SERVES 6**

This salad is composed of several elements commonly used in Korean cuisine: persimmons, pomegranates, pine nuts, and Korean mustard. The two main types of persimmon are crisp, squat *dan gam* (Fuyu), eaten while still firm, and heart-shaped *hongsi* (Hachiya), which should only be eaten when they feel soft and bloated like a water balloon. Both are sold by the case in Korean markets. Buy *hongsi* when they're still firm and let them ripen at home.

6 cups tightly packed chopped frisée
(about 5 ounces)

3 firm but ripe *dan gam* (Fuyu) persimmons, peeled and cut into thin wedges

½ cup pomegranate seeds

⅓ cup pine nuts, toasted

2 ounces feta cheese, crumbled
(about ¼ cup)

2 tablespoons finely chopped fresh chives

1 recipe Spicy Korean Mustard Vinaigrette
(page 217)

Kosher salt or sea salt

Freshly ground black pepper

IN A LARGE BOWL, combine the frisée, persimmons, pomegranate seeds, half the pine nuts, the feta cheese, and the chives. Drizzle with the vinaigrette, season with salt and pepper, and toss gently to coat. Sprinkle with the remaining pine nuts and serve immediately.

TIP: *To remove the seeds from a pomegranate without staining everything around you, cut off the top and bottom and then score the sides from top to bottom in four or five places, evenly spacing the cuts. Set the pomegranate in a large bowl of water and pull it apart where it's scored. Loosen the seeds with your fingers under the water, discarding the peels and the white pith that floats to the top of the water. Strain out the seeds and remove any remaining pith.*

# ROASTED KOREAN SWEET POTATOES

## *GUN GOGUMA*

**SERVES 2**

You'll often see street vendors in Korea roasting these spuds in the winter. My dad loves eating these as a snack on their own. Sometimes I'll roast more sweet potatoes than I need and eat them cold from the fridge when I'm feeling peckish.

Korean sweet potatoes are usually sweet enough that you don't need any toppings, but a pinch of salt is a nice touch. The skins are edible, too, although they peel off easily if you'd rather not eat them. I like to pick potatoes that are long, thin, and evenly shaped, as opposed to those that are blocky or lumpy, as they cook quicker and more evenly.

**2 (9- to 10-ounce) Korean sweet potatoes**

**Kosher salt or sea salt (optional)**

PREHEAT THE OVEN to 400°F.

Wrap each sweet potato in aluminum foil. Roast, turning halfway through, until easily pierced with the tip of a knife, 1 to 1½ hours total. Let cool slightly before serving with salt, if desired.

TIP: *For a sweet twist, try adding brown sugar and a little butter—your potato will transform into a dessert.*

# ZUCCHINI RIBBONS

*HOBAK BOKKEUM*

**SERVES 4**

I serve this dish with Steamed Ginger Sea Bass (page 148), but it also makes a terrific side to pretty much any fish or meat dish, as well as a very nice *banchan*. Definitely try to find the salted shrimp, if you can, as it makes a big impact on the flavor.

3 medium zucchini

1 tablespoon vegetable oil

1 clove garlic, grated or minced

1 teaspoon salted shrimp (*saewoo jeot*), rinsed and coarsely chopped, or 4 anchovy fillets packed in oil, drained and coarsely chopped

1 tablespoon mirin

Large pinch of finely chopped fresh chives, for serving (optional)

USING A WIDE vegetable peeler or mandoline, thinly slice the zucchini lengthwise into long ribbons about ⅛ inch thick; set aside. In a large skillet, heat the oil over medium-high heat. Add the garlic and shrimp and cook, stirring often, until the garlic is just softened, about 30 seconds. Add the zucchini and cook, tossing gently, until just wilted, about 3 minutes. Add the mirin and cook until the zucchini is soft, about 1 minute more. Transfer the zucchini to a platter and sprinkle with the chives, if desired.

# GRILLED CORN ON THE COB

*WITH DOENJANG BUTTER*

**SERVES 4**

Coming from New Jersey, the Garden State, I'm a sucker for fresh-picked corn on the cob during the summer. I like to serve this grilled corn with just about any barbecue, but especially with my Mom's BBQ Chicken (page 174). The butter is good on steamed corn, too.

**4 tablespoons (½ stick) unsalted butter, at room temperature**

**1 tablespoon *doenjang* (Korean soybean paste)**

**½ scallion, thinly sliced on an angle**

**Vegetable oil, for grilling**

**4 ears corn, shucked**

PREHEAT A GAS or charcoal grill to medium.

In a small bowl, whisk together the butter and soybean paste until smooth. Stir in the scallion and set aside. Lightly brush the grill grates with oil. Grill the corn, turning occasionally, until charred in spots, about 10 minutes. Transfer the corn to a platter and slather with the *doenjang* butter, or serve the butter on the side. Serve immediately.

# GRILLED TWIST PEPPERS

*GWARI GOCHU GUI*

**SERVES 4**

Korean twist peppers are related to shishito and Padrón peppers and are especially good grilled. They can be sneaky: most are mild, but once in a while you come across a very spicy one. These make a great plate for guests to snack on before the main meal arrives.

**¾ pound Korean twist peppers (*gwari gochu*), shishito, or Padrón peppers**

**1 tablespoon vegetable oil**

**Flaky sea salt, such as Maldon**

**Pinch of *gochugaru* (Korean chile flakes; optional)**

PREHEAT A GAS or charcoal grill to medium-hot.

In a medium bowl, toss together the peppers and oil. Arrange the peppers on the grill without crowding and taking care not to drop them through the grate. Set the bowl aside. Grill the peppers, covered, until blistered and slightly charred, 1½ to 2 minutes. Flip them and cook for 1 minute more. Return the peppers to the bowl and season with salt and the chile flakes (if using).

# DOENJANG-GLAZED BROILED ASIAN EGGPLANT

*DOENJANG GAJI GUI*

**SERVES 6**

This eggplant recipe is a variation of the Japanese version, *nasu dengaku*, which is an all-time fave for me. Here I use *doenjang*, which kicks the flavor up a notch. It is divine!

3 Asian eggplants (about 5 ounces each), halved lengthwise

Vegetable oil, for broiling

Kosher salt or sea salt

Freshly ground black pepper

½ cup Doenjang Glaze (page 216)

Roasted sesame seeds, for serving

Pinch of *gochugaru* (Korean chile flakes), for serving (optional)

Handful of scallions, thinly sliced on an angle, for serving

PREHEAT THE BROILER and position a rack 4 to 5 inches from the heat source. Line a baking sheet with aluminum foil.

Score the flesh of each eggplant half in a cross-hatch pattern, cutting deeply but not all the way through to the skin. Brush the eggplant halves with oil and season with salt and pepper. Arrange them, skin-side up, in a single layer on the prepared baking sheet.

Broil until the skins start to discolor in spots and the eggplants soften a bit, 3 to 5 minutes. Flip them and continue to broil until the cut sides are lightly golden and the eggplants are soft when squeezed, 3 to 5 minutes more. Spread the glaze over the flesh and broil until it's bubbling and lightly charred in spots, about 5 minutes more. Watch carefully, as the glaze can burn quickly. Transfer the eggplant to plates, flesh-side up, and garnish with sesame seeds, chile flakes, if desired, and the scallions.

TIP: *While the eggplant halves look nicer served as is, cutting them into smaller pieces makes them easier to eat.*

RICE

# STEAMED WHITE RICE
*BAP*

**MAKES ABOUT 6 CUPS**

Almost every Korean meal starts with steamed pearly white rice. It is the element that grounds and completes the rest of the meal. One can make a whole meal simply by pairing a bowl of rice with some kimchi or seasoned vegetables and roasted seaweed to wrap it all together. Or it can be part of a much more elaborate meal. It's eaten with stews, soupy broths, and stir-fries, and as the base of rice bowls (bibimbap) topped with various vegetables and proteins. Unless I'm having noodles, my meal does not feel complete without rice. It is such an essential part of eating that Koreans will literally say, "Have you eaten rice?" to ask if you have eaten a meal. It is sustenance, and porcelain-white rice has always been the coveted form (as opposed to its brown counterpart). As a kid, my father used to say that every grain of rice left on my plate would become a pockmark on my face. Out of fear, I made sure I ate every last kernel.

These days, many Koreans make rice—generally short- or medium-grain varieties—in electric rice cookers. These handy gadgets have come a long way from the simple on/off-switch models. Armed with fuzzy logic, they now have the ability to cook different kinds of rice (white, brown, mixed-grain, wild, etc.), various grains, and porridge, too. Some of them even sing and play music! However, it's always good to know how to make rice in a saucepan on the stove. Here's the simple method I use; you don't even need to wait for the water to boil before covering the pot.

**2 cups short- or medium-grain Korean rice**

IN KOREA, we always wash our rice to remove the excess starch. In a medium saucepan with a tight-fitting lid, combine the rice and enough cold tap water to cover it. Swish the rice around with one hand until the water becomes cloudy and then slowly pour the water out, using your hand to keep the rice from falling out of the pot. Repeat two or three more times, until the water runs mostly clear; drain well.

Add 2 cups of water (add up to ¼ cup more if you like softer rice). Steam, covered, over medium-low heat until all the water has been absorbed, about 30 minutes. It's important to refrain from lifting the lid while the rice cooks. I like to set a timer so I can go about my business and not worry about forgetting it. Remove the saucepan from the heat and let it sit, covered and undisturbed, for 10 minutes. Uncover the pot and gently fold the rice over itself with a rice paddle or rubber spatula a few times before serving.

TIP: *The cloudy water from rinsing rice can be used to wash your face and hair. Rice water helps keeps your skin porcelain white and young looking, and your hair healthy and shiny.*

# MIXED RICE BOWL WITH BEEF

## *BIBIMBAP*

### SERVES 4 TO 6

Bibimbap is one of my favorite dishes because I love eating vegetables. It's also very healthy. I always think that two-thirds of your plate should be covered with veggies. The variety of vegetables doesn't really matter too much—use whatever you have. Chopped lettuce leaves or cucumber add a nice crunch, too. The cooking of this dish goes very quickly, so be sure you have all the ingredients ready before you start. (It might seem silly to cook the vegetables separately, but it makes a big difference in the finished dish.) I've simplified this version slightly by making one seasoning mix for all of the vegetables. Traditionally, each vegetable would be seasoned individually. It does better keep the integrity of the flavors, but it is tedious. I've compromised by cooking each one separately, but using the same seasoning. I also make one giant one to share—as that's easier too.

2 tablespoons toasted sesame oil

5 cups Steamed White Rice (page 106)

3 tablespoons soy sauce

3 tablespoons mirin

2 cloves garlic, grated or minced

1 teaspoon grated peeled fresh ginger

1 teaspoon crushed roasted sesame seeds

¼ pound very thinly sliced beef *bulgogi* meat (sold at Korean markets) or rib eye

2 teaspoons sugar

Vegetable oil, for frying

1 cup soybean sprouts, tails and any soft or brown pieces removed, rinsed and dried well

¼ pound shiitake mushrooms, stemmed and cut into ¼-inch slices

½ medium zucchini, thinly sliced on an angle

1 cup snow peas

1 carrot, julienned

6 cups baby spinach

½ cup drained chopped Cabbage Kimchi (page 28)

For Serving:

Gochujang Sauce (page 214)

3 large egg yolks or fried eggs

Black sesame seeds

Radish sprouts (optional)

HEAT A LARGE heavy-bottomed skillet (preferably cast iron) over medium heat. Add 1 tablespoon of the sesame oil and gently spread the rice over the bottom of the skillet in a loose layer. Cook, undisturbed, until the bottom of the rice develops a golden crust, 8 to 10 minutes. This should be about the same time the toppings are done, but if the rice is ready beforehand, just turn off the heat.

Meanwhile, in a small bowl, stir together the soy sauce, 2 tablespoons of the mirin, the remaining 1 tablespoon sesame oil, the garlic, ginger, and sesame seeds. Mix 2 tablespoons of the sauce with the beef and sugar and set aside. Set the remaining seasoning sauce by the stove.

As each vegetable topping is finished, arrange it on a section of the rice in the skillet so the toppings resemble the spokes of a bicycle wheel. In a medium nonstick skillet, heat ½ teaspoon of vegetable oil over medium-high heat. Add the bean sprouts and 1 teaspoon of the seasoning sauce and cook, stirring, until crisp-tender, about 30 seconds. Arrange the bean sprouts on a section of the rice.

Heat 2 teaspoons of oil in the skillet, add the beef, and cook until cooked through, 1 to 2 minutes. Arrange the beef on the rice.

Heat 1 tablespoon of oil in the skillet, add the mushrooms and 1 tablespoon of the sauce, and cook until tender, 1 minute. Arrange the mushrooms on the rice.

Heat ½ teaspoon of oil in the skillet, add the zucchini and 2 teaspoons of the sauce, and cook until just tender, about 1 minute. Arrange the zucchini on the rice.

Heat ½ teaspoon of oil in the skillet, add the snow peas and 2 teaspoons of the sauce, and cook until crisp-tender, 45 seconds. Arrange the snow peas on the rice.

Heat ½ teaspoon of oil in the skillet, add the carrot and 1 teaspoon of the sauce, and cook until crisp-tender, 30 seconds. Arrange the carrot on the rice.

Finally, heat 1 teaspoon oil in the skillet, add the spinach and 1 tablespoon of the sauce, and cook until just wilted, 30 seconds. Arrange the spinach on the rice.

Deglaze the pan with the remaining 1 tablespoon mirin, scrape up any browned bits from the bottom, and spoon the juices from the skillet over the meat on the rice. Arrange the kimchi on a section of the rice.

Spoon the Gochujang Sauce on the center of the rice or serve on the side, if you like. Make a little well in the spinach, mushrooms, and beef and gently put an egg yolk into each or arrange the fried eggs, if using, over the dish. Sprinkle the bibimbap with black sesame seeds and radish sprouts, if desired. Bring the skillet to the table, set it on a trivet, and mix everything together before spooning into bowls.

# DIY MESSY CRAB SEAWEED RICE ROLL

## *GAE KIMBAP*

**SERVES 4 TO 6**

Invite friends over and serve this fun do-it-yourself dish. You can put anything inside the seaweed packages, from tuna salad to cold cuts to kimchi. I often set out seasoned crab meat, omelet strips, and a variety of vegetables and let guests mix and match as they like. Traditionally, the ingredients are rolled in the seaweed, but my version is "messy" because the seaweed's just loosely folded over everything.

Crab:

**2 tablespoons mirin**

**2 tablespoons toasted sesame oil**

**2 cloves garlic, grated or minced**

**2 teaspoons grated peeled fresh ginger**

**2 teaspoons crushed roasted sesame seeds**

**Kosher salt or sea salt**

**8 ounces crabmeat, picked through**

Eggs:

**2 teaspoons vegetable oil**

**Generous pinch of kosher salt or sea salt**

**4 large eggs, lightly beaten with a splash of water**

Dressing:

**2 tablespoons mirin**

**1 tablespoon toasted sesame oil**

**1 tablespoon soy sauce**

**1 teaspoon sugar**

**1 teaspoon black sesame seeds**

**Kosher salt or sea salt**

Vegetables:

**1 (10-ounce) package baby spinach**

**2 carrots, julienned**

**1 (3½-ounce) package enoki mushrooms**

**1 small Kirby cucumber, julienned**

**6 ounces sweet yellow radish pickle (*danmuji*), julienned**

**4 cups Steamed White Rice (page 106)**

**1 tablespoon roasted sesame seeds**

**4 (.14-ounce) individual packets roasted seaweed (*kim*)**

For Serving (optional):

**Dried chile threads (*silgochu*)**

***Gochugaru* (Korean chile flakes)**

**Black sesame seeds**

FOR THE CRAB: In a medium bowl, stir together the mirin, sesame oil, garlic, ginger, sesame seeds, and salt to taste. Add the crab and gently toss to coat. Cover and let marinate in the refrigerator while you prepare the rest of the dish.

FOR THE EGGS: In a medium nonstick skillet, heat the oil over medium heat. Beat the salt into the eggs and then add the egg mixture to the skillet, swirling to evenly coat the bottom. Cook, without touching, until the egg is set but just barely browned on the bottom, about 2 minutes. Flip and continue to cook until the bottom is set, again trying not to get too much color on the egg, 15 to 20 seconds more. Slide onto a cutting board, carefully roll into a log, and cut crosswise into ½-inch-wide strips. Set the egg strips aside.

FOR THE DRESSING: In a small bowl, stir together the mirin, sesame oil, soy sauce, sugar, black sesame seeds, and salt to taste until the sugar and salt have dissolved. Set the dressing aside.

FOR THE VEGETABLES: Bring a large pot of salted water to a boil and prepare an ice water bath. Blanch the spinach in the boiling water until just wilted and then shock in the ice water bath. Drain well and squeeze out any excess water. In a medium bowl, toss together the spinach and half the dressing. In another medium bowl, toss together the carrots and the remaining dressing.

Arrange the crabmeat, egg strips, spinach, carrots, enoki, cucumber, and pickled daikon in separate piles on a platter or in individual bowls. Put the rice in a serving bowl and sprinkle with the roasted sesame seeds. Put the seaweed on a plate. As for the optional garnishes, I particularly like to top the crab with chile threads, the egg with chile flakes, and the carrots and cucumbers with black sesame seeds, but they're great without them, too.

Now comes the fun part: Everyone makes their own kimbap. Put a piece of seaweed in one hand with the short sides running up and down. Top with a spoonful of rice, followed by the ingredients of your choice, arranging them crosswise. Use just one or mix a few together. Next, gather the short ends of the seaweed together to form a loose roll and eat.

# RAW FISH AND SALAD RICE BOWLS

*HWE DUP BAP*

**SERVES 4**

This very refreshing dish is a kicked-up version of *chirashi*, a Japanese classic in which seasoned rice is "scattered" with a variety of raw fish/seafood and vegetables/garnishes. Use whatever fish/seafood you like as long as it is super fresh. For a fresh vegetarian rice bowl, substitute panfried tofu for the fish and /or seafood.

## Sauce:

**6 tablespoons *gochujang* (Korean chile paste)**

**4½ teaspoons rice vinegar**

**4½ teaspoons honey**

**1 teaspoon toasted sesame oil**

**1 teaspoon roasted sesame seeds**

**1 clove garlic, grated or minced**

## Rice Bowls:

**4 cups Steamed White Rice (page 106)**

**3 cups chopped red- or green-leaf lettuce**

**1 carrot, julienned**

**½ English cucumber, seeded and julienned**

**4 ounces Korean white radish (*mu*) or daikon, peeled and julienned**

**1 (2½-ounce) package radish sprouts**

**1½ pounds assorted sashimi-quality fish and/or seafood, such as fluke, salmon, tuna, yellowtail, octopus, and scallops, cut into bite-size pieces**

**¼ cup flying fish roe**

## For Serving:

**Roasted seaweed (*kim*), julienned**

**4 perilla leaves (*ggaennip*), also known as sesame leaves, torn (optional)**

**Roasted and black sesame seeds**

FOR THE SAUCE: In a small bowl, whisk together all the sauce ingredients until smooth, divide among four small dishes, and set aside.

FOR THE RICE BOWLS: Divide the rice among four bowls large enough so that everything can be mixed together. Arrange the lettuce, carrot, cucumber, radish, and radish sprouts in bunches on top of the rice. Top with the fish and/or seafood, keeping the same types together, followed by a tablespoon of the fish roe. Scatter the rice bowls with the seaweed, perilla leaves (if using), and sesame seeds and serve with the sauce. People can add as much sauce as they like before mixing together all the ingredients.

# KIMCHI FRIED RICE

## *KIMCHI BOKKEUM BAP*

**SERVES 4**

My sister used to make this for me when we lived together in New York, and I loved it! Fried rice is the perfect way to use up leftovers, so feel free to improvise. Any kind of veggies or meat you have in the fridge—just toss them in. This is a great lunch or side dish. A variation, called *omurice*, is to make omelets with the eggs and wrap them around the fried rice like a burrito. At Jinjuu, we like to fancy up our kimchi fried rice with a garnish of julienned roasted seaweed (*kim*) and lotus root chips.

2 tablespoons vegetable oil

2 slices thick-cut bacon, diced

2 carrots, diced

1 clove garlic, grated or minced

9 button mushrooms, stemmed and diced

½ zucchini, diced

3 scallions, thinly sliced on an angle

1 cup drained Cabbage Kimchi (page 28), chopped

4 cups Steamed White Rice (page 106), at room temperature

Kosher salt or sea salt

Freshly ground black pepper

4 soft sunny-side-up fried eggs

**IN A LARGE SKILLET,** heat the oil over medium-high heat. Add the bacon and cook, stirring occasionally, until crispy, about 2 minutes. Using a slotted spoon, transfer the bacon to a paper towel–lined plate to drain.

Reduce the heat to medium, add the carrots and garlic, and cook, stirring continuously, until the carrots are just softened, 2 to 3 minutes. Add the mushrooms, zucchini, two-thirds of the scallions, and the kimchi and cook until the vegetables are tender, 4 to 5 minutes. Add the rice and drained bacon, breaking up the rice with a wooden spoon and combining it with the other ingredients. Cook, stirring occasionally, until the rice is hot, about 5 minutes. Season with salt and pepper. Spoon the fried rice into four bowls and top each with a fried egg and the remaining scallions.

*TIP: Kimchi can stain your cutting board and the smell has a habit of lingering, too. To avoid this, put the kimchi in a bowl and use kitchen shears to cut it into smaller pieces.*

# NOODLES

# ICE-COLD NOODLES

## *NAENGMYUN*

**SERVES 2**

This totally addictive dish is from North Korea, where my dad is from, so it's dear to his heart. My mom used to make it for him in the summertime, and I can still remember the slurping noises at the dinner table when it was served. *Naengmyun* noodles are the best, as they contain buckwheat and sweet potato, which gives them a great springy texture. They're also thinner than regular buckwheat noodles, which make them perfect for slurping. The "salad" that I created to go on top is a real crowd-pleaser. Make more to serve on the side, if you like.

Noodles:

**2 cups beef stock**

**¼ teaspoon superfine sugar**

**1 to 2 tablespoons rice vinegar**

**Pinch of kosher salt or sea salt**

**7 ounces Korean buckwheat–sweet potato noodles (naengmyun)**

Salad:

**¾ cup julienned unpeeled Asian pear or other firm but ripe pear**

**2 tablespoons julienned unpeeled cucumber**

**2 tablespoons julienned red onion, soaked in ice water for 10 minutes and then drained**

**1 tablespoon rice vinegar**

**½ teaspoon superfine sugar**

**½ teaspoon prepared Korean mustard (gyeoja) or English mustard**

**Pinch of kosher salt or sea salt**

For Serving:

**2 ounces sliced cooked roast beef, cut into 1½-inch-wide pieces**

**2 large eggs, hard-boiled, peeled, and halved or quartered lengthwise**

**Freshly ground black pepper**

**Roasted sesame seeds**

**Roasted seaweed (kim), julienned**

FOR THE NOODLES: Prepare an ice water bath. In a medium saucepan, heat the stock with the sugar over low heat, stirring until the sugar has dissolved. Stir in 1 tablespoon of the vinegar and the salt, adding more vinegar to taste. Remove from the heat, pour into a heatproof container, and chill over the ice water bath. While the soup is chilling, make the noodles according to the instructions on the package. Rinse well with cold water, massaging to remove excess starch. Drain and set aside.

FOR THE SALAD: In a small bowl, toss together all the salad ingredients. Divide the noodles between two bowls. (Add some crushed ice to the bottom of the bowls to keep the noodles well chilled, if you like.) Pour the cold broth over the noodles. Top the noodles with the salad. Divide the roast beef and eggs between the bowls. Grind pepper over each egg and sprinkle with sesame seeds and seaweed.

TIP: *Add some* dongchimi *broth from Radish Water Kimchi (page 40) to give this stock great flavor and an even more refreshing quality.*

# STIR-FRIED SWEET POTATO NOODLES

## *JAPCHAE*

**SERVES 6**

My mom used to make this dish for dinner parties, so it always has a special-occasion feel for me. I love the springiness of Korean sweet potato noodles (which, by the way, are gluten-free), but they sometimes get a little long and/or tangled. If that happens, just cut them with kitchen scissors after cooking and rinsing them. Traditionally, this dish is made with beef; here I've used shrimp, but you can substitute any protein, including tofu, scallops, or chicken. At Jinjuu, our version with shrimp is a best seller.

Noodles:

**1 pound sweet potato noodles (*dangmyun*)**

**2 tablespoons soy sauce**

Eggs:

**1 teaspoon vegetable oil**

**Pinch of kosher salt or sea salt**

**2 large eggs, lightly beaten with a splash of water**

Shrimp:

**1 tablespoon vegetable oil**

**2 large cloves garlic, grated or minced**

**24 jumbo shrimp, peeled (including tails, if desired) and deveined, and patted dry**

**Kosher salt or sea salt**

**1 tablespoon mirin**

Vegetables:

**1 tablespoon vegetable oil**

**1 large onion, thinly sliced**

**12 cremini, button, or shiitake mushrooms, stemmed and sliced**

**1 large carrot, julienned**

**1 (5-ounce) package baby spinach**

**3 scallions, cut into 2-inch pieces**

Sauce:

**2 tablespoons sugar**

**2 tablespoons toasted sesame oil**

**2 tablespoons crushed roasted sesame seeds**

**1 tablespoon soy sauce**

**2 teaspoons kosher salt or sea salt**

For Serving:

**½ scallion, cut lengthwise into thin strips, soaked in ice water until curled, and then drained**

**Black sesame seeds**

FOR THE NOODLES: Bring a large pot of water to a boil. Add the noodles and cook according to the package directions until soft. Briefly rinse in cold water and then drain well. Transfer to a large bowl, toss with the soy sauce until coated, and set aside.

FOR THE EGGS: In a medium nonstick skillet, heat the oil over medium heat. Beat the salt into the eggs, then add the egg mixture to the skillet, swirling to evenly coat the bottom. Cook, without touching, until the egg is set but just barely browned on the bottom, about 2 minutes. Flip and continue to cook until the bottom is set, again trying not to get too much color on the egg, 15 to 20 seconds more. Slide onto a cutting board, carefully roll into a log, and cut crosswise into thin strips. Set the egg strips aside and wipe out the skillet.

FOR THE SHRIMP: Add the oil to the skillet and heat over medium-high heat. Add the garlic and cook, stirring often, until fragrant, about 10 seconds. Don't let the garlic brown. Add the shrimp, season with salt, and cook, stirring often, until the shrimp are barely pink, about 1½ minutes. Add the mirin and cook, stirring often, until the shrimp are cooked through, about 3 minutes more. Transfer the shrimp mixture to a bowl.

FOR THE VEGETABLES: In the same skillet, heat the oil over medium heat. Add the onion and cook, stirring often, until slightly softened, about 1 minute. Add any juices from the bowl of shrimp and toss to coat. Add the mushrooms and carrot and cook until slightly softened. Add the spinach in handfuls, tossing with the other ingredients and adding more as it wilts. Cook until all the spinach is wilted, 2 to 3 minutes. Add the scallions and drained noodles and toss together.

FOR THE SAUCE: Add the sugar, sesame oil, sesame seeds, soy sauce, and salt to the skillet. Toss well and cook until the noodles are heated through and glossy, about 2 minutes. Add the egg strips and shrimp and gently toss.

Transfer to a platter, top with the scallion curls and sesame seeds, and serve immediately.

# INSTANT NOODLES WITH SPICY RICE CAKES AND FISH CAKES

## *RA-BOKKI*

**SERVES 4 TO 6**

*Ra-bokki* is a combination of *ramyun* (Korean for ramen noodles) and *dduk bokki*, spicy-sweet and saucy stir-fried rice cakes, two of the most famous and popular Korean street foods. Together, they're like a little bit of dirty naughty eating for me, which I love. You can use any brand of *ramyun/ramen* noodles, but I'm partial to Shin Ramyun.

15 large dried anchovies (*myulchi*), head and guts removed

1 (4-inch-long) piece dried kelp (*dashima*)

2 carrots, thinly sliced on an angle

1 onion, thinly sliced

2 cloves garlic, grated or minced

¼ cup *gochujang* (Korean chile paste)

2 tablespoons sugar

1 tablespoon *gochugaru* (Korean chile flakes)

1 tablespoon soy sauce

3 cups chopped napa or Korean cabbage

1 package instant *ramyun*/ramen noodles, seasoning packet discarded

1 pound 2-inch-long cylindrical rice cakes (*dduk*), soaked in cold water for 15 to 30 minutes and then drained

7 ounces fish cake sheets (*eomuk*), cut into triangular pieces about 3 inches long

2 teaspoons toasted sesame oil

1 tablespoon roasted sesame seeds

2 to 3 large eggs, hard-boiled, peeled, and halved or quartered lengthwise

Handful of scallions, thinly sliced on an angle, for serving

IN A MEDIUM saucepan, combine the anchovies, kelp, and 5 cups water and bring to a boil. Reduce the heat to maintain a simmer for about 20 minutes. Pass the anchovy stock through a fine-mesh strainer into a large, wide, deep skillet and discard the solids.

Return the stock to maintain a simmer. Add the carrots, onion, garlic, chile paste, sugar, chile flakes, and soy sauce, stir to combine, and simmer for 5 minutes. Add the cabbage and noodles and simmer, stirring often, until the noodles are slightly softened, about 2 minutes more.

Add the rice cakes and fish cakes and cook, stirring occasionally, until the noodles are just tender and the sauce has thickened slightly, about 5 minutes more. Drizzle with the sesame oil, sprinkle with the sesame seeds, and nestle the eggs in the sauce. Serve immediately, topped with the scallions.

# LATE-NIGHT NAUGHTY NOODLES

*RAMYUN*

**MAKES 1 LARGE SERVING**

Sometimes nothing hits the spot better than instant *ramyun* (Korean for ramen) and a cold beer. Switching out the seasoning packet for some flavored stock, though, makes it much tastier and more healthful. I also like to build it into a proper meal by pimping it out with some frozen shrimp or dumplings (although you can certainly use fresh, too), veggies, meat—whatever I have on hand. Feel free to adjust the spice level to your taste.

3 cups chicken stock

2 teaspoons *gochujang* (Korean chile paste)

1 teaspoon *doenjang* (Korean soybean paste)

1 teaspoon *gochugaru* (Korean chile flakes), plus more for serving (optional)

1 small fresh Korean red chile or Fresno chile, thinly sliced on an angle

1 package instant *ramyun*/ramen noodles, seasoning packet discarded

5 large peeled and deveined frozen shrimp

Handful of sugar snap peas or baby spinach

½ cup coarsely shredded cooked chicken

1 scallion, cut into 2-inch pieces, plus a large pinch of thinly sliced scallions for serving (optional)

1 large egg

Freshly ground black pepper (optional)

IN A MEDIUM saucepan, combine the stock, chile paste, soybean paste, chile flakes, and chile and bring to a boil over high heat, whisking occasionally to dissolve the soybean paste.

Open the package of noodles and, keeping the noodles in the bag, break them in half crosswise. Put both halves into the boiling stock mixture. (I love to eat any remaining bits of noodles by shaking them from the bag into my mouth.) Add the shrimp and sugar snap peas (if using; if you're using spinach, wait until the next step).

Bring the broth back to a boil and add the chicken and scallion. When the noodles are almost done, about 5 minutes total, add the spinach (if using) and stir to wilt. Crack the egg into the saucepan and let it poach, or give it a gentle stir to break it up and form egg ribbons. Eat your noodles straight from the pot, or if you're feeling fancy, transfer to a bowl and garnish with the sliced scallions, more chile flakes, and pepper.

# NOODLES WITH BLACK BEAN SAUCE

## *JJAJANGMYUN*

**SERVES 4 TO 6**

Both Korean and Chinese restaurants have a version of this Korean-Chinese dish, with the Korean version being saucier and the Chinese version being drier. Consider yourself warned: the black bean sauce is very messy and even the most elegant diner will be hard-pressed to stay clean. For even cooking and a nice presentation, cut all the vegetables into half-inch dice. Note: Do not substitute Chinese black bean sauce here, as it is completely different.

2 tablespoons potato starch

3 tablespoons vegetable oil

10 ounces skinless pork belly, cut into ¼-inch cubes

1½ cups diced onions

3 cloves garlic, grated or minced

1 teaspoon grated peeled fresh ginger

1½ cups diced peeled potatoes

1 cup diced zucchini

½ cup diced daikon radish

⅔ cup black bean paste (*chunjang*)

1 teaspoon brown sugar

1 teaspoon kosher salt or sea salt

Freshly ground black pepper

17 ounces fresh Chinese-style wheat noodles (*jjajangmyun*)

Large handful of seeded and julienned cucumber, for serving

Toasted sesame oil, for serving

Roasted sesame seeds, for serving

IN A SMALL BOWL, combine the potato starch and ¼ cup water and set aside.

In a large nonstick skillet, heat the vegetable oil over medium-high heat. Add the pork and cook, stirring often, until it is browned on all sides and some of its fat has rendered out, 6 to 7 minutes. Add the onions, garlic, and ginger and cook, stirring occasionally, until the onions have softened, about 5 minutes. Add the potatoes, zucchini, and radish and cook, stirring occasionally, until the radish and potato start to turn translucent, 5 to 6 minutes.

Stir in the black bean paste, brown sugar, salt, and pepper to taste. Add 3 cups water and mix well. Simmer gently for 3 to 4 minutes. Stir the potato starch mixture, add it to the skillet, and mix well. Simmer, stirring frequently, until the vegetables are cooked through and the sauce has thickened, 10 to 12 minutes more.

Meanwhile, cook the noodles according to the package instructions (usually 5 to 7 minutes), drain, rinse well, and drain again. Divide the noodles among four to six large bowls. Spoon the vegetable mixture on top of the noodles and garnish with the cucumber, sesame oil, and sesame seeds.

# SPICY SEAFOOD NOODLE SOUP

*JJAMBBONG*

**SERVES 4**

This very brothy Korean-Chinese soup can easily be stretched to serve six—just bulk it up with more noodles, seafood, and veggies. Don't be intimidated by the long ingredients list; it's really an easy dish to put together and the denouement is divine!

Stock:

1 (8-ounce) bottle clam juice

½ small onion, thinly sliced

8 large dried anchovies (*myulchi*), head and guts removed

3 dried shiitake mushrooms

1 (4-inch-long) piece dried kelp (*dashima*)

Soup:

12 ounces fresh Chinese-style wheat noodles (*jjajangmyun*)

4 squid bodies, rinsed and patted dry

3 tablespoons vegetable oil

6 large cloves garlic, grated or minced

4 scallions, cut into 2-inch pieces

3 tablespoons *gochugaru* (Korean chile flakes)

2 tablespoons soy sauce

½ tablespoon grated peeled fresh ginger

4 ounces pork tenderloin, thinly sliced

1 carrot, cut on an angle into ½-inch slices

5 large napa or Korean cabbage leaves, cut into ½-inch slices

½ small zucchini, halved lengthwise and cut into ½-inch slices

½ small onion, thinly sliced

5 shiitake mushrooms, stemmed and cut into ½-inch slices

1 dozen littleneck clams, cleaned

8 mussels, cleaned and debearded

8 large shrimp, peeled and deveined

Kosher salt or sea salt

Freshly ground black pepper

For Serving:

Toasted sesame oil

Handful of fresh chives, cut into 1-inch pieces

FOR THE STOCK: In a medium saucepan, combine the clam juice, onion, dried anchovies, mushrooms, kelp, and 10 cups water and bring to a boil over high heat. Reduce the heat to maintain a simmer and cook for 30 minutes. Pass the anchovy stock through a fine-mesh strainer into a large bowl and discard the solids. Set the stock aside.

FOR THE SOUP: Cook the noodles according to the package instructions (usually 5 to 7 minutes) and drain. Set aside.

Cut the squid bodies open, lay them flat, and score in a crosshatch pattern, being careful not to cut through the flesh. Cut the bodies lengthwise into 2-inch-wide strips and set the squid aside.

In a large heavy-bottomed pot, heat the oil over medium heat. Add the garlic, scallions, chile flakes, soy sauce, and ginger and cook, stirring, until the scallions wilt slightly, about 30 seconds.

Add the pork and cook until it just loses its pinkness, about 1 minute. Add the carrot, cabbage, zucchini, onion, and mushrooms and cook, stirring often, until the vegetables are slightly softened, about 2 minutes.

Add the anchovy stock and bring to a boil over high heat. Add the clams, reduce the heat, and simmer, covered, for 4 minutes. Add the mussels, cover, and simmer until the clam and mussels have opened, 5 to 6 minutes more. Add the

shrimp, stir, and cook for 1 minute more. Add the squid, stir, and cook until opaque, about 30 seconds more. Discard any clams and mussels that haven't opened. Stir in the cooked noodles, season with salt and pepper, and heat through.

Drizzle with sesame oil, sprinkle with the chives, and serve immediately.

# HAND-TORN NOODLE SOUP

## *SUJEBI*

**SERVES 4**

This is a dish that is offered at restaurants when a pot of soup is served at the table, kept warm on top of a burner. A ball of dough is brought to the table toward the end of the meal, and diners tear off pieces, stretch them thin, and throw them into the pot to cook. This is especially fun for the kids. The stretched-out dough doesn't have to be any specific shape, just as long as it's thin. This can be made with pretty much any kind of brothy soup. I have many fond memories of making *sujebi* with my mom and smacking on the toothsome dough "noodles."

**Dough:**

**2 cups all-purpose flour**

**1 tablespoon vegetable oil**

**1 teaspoon sugar**

**½ teaspoon kosher salt or sea salt**

**Soup:**

**8 large dried anchovies (*myulchi*), head and guts removed**

**1 (5-inch-long) piece dried kelp (*dashima*)**

**2 tablespoons fish sauce**

**¾ pound Yukon Gold potatoes, halved lengthwise and cut into ½-inch slices**

**1 carrot, cut on an angle into ½-inch slices**

**1 small zucchini, halved lengthwise and cut into ½-inch slices**

**½ small onion, diced**

**4 large cloves garlic, grated or minced**

**Freshly ground black pepper**

**6 ounces baby spinach**

**2 large eggs, lightly beaten**

**2 tablespoons crushed roasted sesame seeds**

**1 tablespoon toasted sesame oil**

**For Serving:**

**Handful of julienned roasted seaweed (*kim*)**

**Handful scallions thinly sliced on an angle**

**FOR THE DOUGH:** In a large bowl, stir together all the dough ingredients with ¾ cup water until a dough forms. Transfer to a clean work surface and knead until smooth, about 5 minutes. Cover with plastic wrap and let rest at room temperature for about 30 minutes.

**FOR THE SOUP:** In a large pot, combine the anchovies, kelp, fish sauce, and 10 cups water and bring to a boil over high heat. Reduce the heat to maintain a simmer for 20 minutes. Pass the anchovy stock through a fine-mesh strainer into another large pot (or transfer to a bowl and return to the same pot) and discard the anchovies. Cut the kelp into ½-inch strips and set aside.

Return the stock to a boil over high heat. Add the kelp strips, potatoes, carrot, zucchini, onion, and garlic, and reduce the heat to maintain a simmer until the vegetables are almost tender, 8 to 10 minutes. Season with pepper.

While the soup is simmering, tear off 1-inch pieces of dough from the ball and stretch them into noodles about ⅛ inch thick. Don't worry if they're randomly shaped—the important thing is that they're thin. Drop the noodles into the soup as you go, repeating until the dough is gone. Simmer until all the noodles are floating, about 5 minutes after the last one is thrown in.

Stir in the spinach and let it wilt just a touch. Slowly add the eggs in a thin stream and then gently mix just once to form delicate egg ribbons. Stir in the sesame seeds and sesame oil.

Serve the soup immediately in bowls and top with the seaweed and scallions.

Noodles

# SOUPS & STEWS

# SOFT TOFU AND VEGETABLE STEW

## *YACHAE SOON DUBU JJIGAE*

**SERVES 4**

This surprisingly addictive spicy tofu stew is perfect for a cold evening. The mushroom stock lends a deep, earthy taste and complexity, while the sweet zucchini and creamy egg cut the heat. There are so many different types of *jjigae*; this is my favorite, although I usually make it with seafood.

### Stock:

**½ onion, coarsely chopped**

**4 dried shiitake mushrooms**

**1 scallion, coarsely chopped**

**1 (5-inch-long) piece dried kelp (*dashima*)**

### Stew:

**1 tablespoon vegetable oil**

**½ onion, diced**

**2 tablespoons *gochugaru* (Korean chile flakes)**

**2 cloves garlic, grated or minced**

**1 teaspoon grated peeled fresh ginger**

**1 small zucchini, halved lengthwise and cut into ½-inch slices**

**2 cups packed baby spinach**

**2 cups sliced assorted mushrooms (button, enoki, oyster, shiitake)**

**1 cup packed thickly sliced Korean or napa cabbage leaves**

**14 ounces soft silken tofu, drained**

**Kosher salt or sea salt**

**1 large egg**

### For Serving:

**Toasted sesame oil**

**Handful of fresh chives, cut into 3-inch pieces**

**Roasted sesame seeds**

FOR THE STOCK: In a large pot, combine the onion, dried mushrooms, scallions, kelp, and 3 cups water and bring to a boil over high heat. Reduce the heat to maintain a simmer and cook, covered, for about 45 minutes. Strain, discarding the solids, and set aside.

FOR THE STEW: In a medium heavy-bottomed saucepan, heat the oil over medium-low heat. Add the onion and chile flakes and cook, stirring occasionally, until the onion is just softened, about 5 minutes. Stir in the garlic and ginger, add the stock, and bring to a simmer over medium-high heat.

Add the zucchini, spinach, fresh mushrooms, and cabbage and bring to a boil. Reduce the heat to maintain a simmer until the vegetables are softened, about 5 minutes. Carefully add the tofu in chunks, season with salt, and gently stir, trying to keep the tofu intact as much as possible. When the tofu is heated through, crack an egg into the saucepan and gently mix it into the stew.

Remove the stew from the heat and top with a drizzle of sesame oil, the chives, and a sprinkle of sesame seeds. Serve in bowls.

TIP: *If you aren't a vegetarian, try adding clams, some clam broth, and even a little bacon to the dish. They all contribute great flavor.*

# DOENJANG STEW

*DOENJANG JJIGAE*

**SERVES 4 TO 6**

There is no shortage of hearty stews in the Korean repertoire of comfort food. This one is both earthy from fermented soybean paste and lots of veggies, and briny from the clams and anchovy-based broth. The tofu soaks up all that good flavor and is particular sought after. There's always the risk of a clam not opening, so feel to add a couple extra to the pot so no one gets shorted.

10 large dried anchovies (*myulchi*), heads and guts removed

1 (4-inch-long) piece dried kelp (*dashima*)

5 to 6 tablespoons *doenjang* (Korean soybean paste)

2 teaspoons *gochugaru* (Korean chile flakes)

1½ teaspoons *gochujang* (Korean chile paste)

1 small zucchini, diced

½ small onion, finely diced

¾ cup peeled diced Korean white radish (*mu*) or daikon

4 cloves garlic, grated or minced

12 littleneck clams, cleaned

14 ounces firm tofu, drained and cut into 1-inch cubes

1 (3½-ounce) package enoki mushrooms, roots trimmed

2 scallions, thinly sliced on an angle

1 fresh Korean red chile or Fresno chile, seeded, if desired, and thinly sliced

1 fresh Korean green chile or jalapeño, seeded, if desired, and thinly sliced on an angle

Toasted sesame oil, for serving

Steamed White Rice (page 106), for serving

IN A MEDIUM heavy-bottomed saucepan, combine the anchovies, kelp, and 4 cups water and bring to a boil over high heat. Reduce the heat to maintain a simmer and cook for 15 to 20 minutes. Pass the anchovy stock through a fine-mesh strainer into another medium heavy-bottomed saucepan (or strain into a bowl and return the stock to the same saucepan) and discard the solids.

Return the stock to a simmer, add 5 tablespoons of the soybean paste, the chile flakes, and the chile paste, and whisk until the soybean paste has dissolved. Taste the stock; if you'd like a stronger soybean paste flavor, whisk in a little more. Add the zucchini, onion, radish, and garlic and simmer until the vegetables are just tender, about 5 minutes more.

Add the clams, cover, and simmer until the clams open, 5 to 7 minutes. Discard any clams that don't open. Add the tofu, mushrooms, scallions, and red and green chiles and simmer, uncovered, until warmed through, about 2 minutes. Lightly drizzle with sesame oil and serve immediately, with rice.

TIP: *There are lots of ways to clean clams, but here's how I usually do it: Put them in a single layer in a colander set in a large bowl. Sprinkle with salt, add enough water to cover, and let sit for 30 to 60 minutes. Lift the clams out of the water, scrub each one well, and then rinse.*

# MAGICAL CHICKEN GINSENG SOUP

*SAMGYETANG*

**SERVES 2**

This medicinal soup can give you an energizing lift and immunity boost. Ginseng has numerous health benefits and this soup is known as the "Korean penicillin." Whenever I'm feeling under the weather, I'll make this and feel warm and cozy in no time. If you use the dried ginseng root, there's no need for the tea, and vice versa, but I have used both together and the result is truly lovely. Find the wishbones when eating this soup and make the dish extra magical by making a wish!

10 (3-gram) packets Korean red ginseng tea

4 large cloves garlic

3 jujube dates, or 15 goji berries

3 pieces dried Korean red ginseng (optional)

2 cooked chestnuts, peeled (optional)

1 cup uncooked sweet rice

2 baby chickens (poussin) or Cornish hens (about 2 pounds each)

Dried chile threads (*silgochu*)

Handful of fresh pea shoots (optional)

Black sesame seeds

Toasted sesame oil

Kosher salt or sea salt

Freshly ground black pepper

BRING 4 CUPS WATER to a boil in a small saucepan. Add the tea and stir until the powder has dissolved; set aside.

Put 2 cloves of garlic, 1 jujube date (or 10 goji berries), 1 piece ginseng (if using), 1 chestnut (if using), and 2 tablespoons of rice into the cavity of each bird. Skewer the cavities closed with a toothpick. Put the remaining ¾ cup rice in a double layer of cheesecloth with the remaining jujube date (or 5 goji berries) and 1 piece ginseng (if using). Tie the cloth closed, but leave space for the rice to expand.

Put the chickens and the rice bag into a large, wide, heavy-bottomed pot. Pour the tea over the chickens, top off with enough water to cover, if needed, and bring to a boil over high heat. Reduce the heat to maintain a simmer, and cook, occasionally skimming off any fat that comes to the surface, until the chickens are cooked through and the legs pull away from the body easily when tugged, about 2 hours.

Carefully transfer the chickens to two bowls and divide the broth between them. Top the chickens with chile threads and the pea shoots, some black sesame seeds, and a drizzle of sesame oil. Unwrap the rice and serve in a separate bowl, sprinkled with more black sesame seeds, if you like. Serve the soup with salt and pepper.

**TIP:** *Korean ginseng, also known as Panax ginseng, is renowned for its high quality and for being the most nutritious. I like to use dried Korean red ginseng when possible. It undergoes a process of steaming and aging, which creates new nutrients that are believed to prevent cancer and obesity. That said, feel free to substitute any quality fresh ginseng in this soup—it's much cheaper and easier to find. In place of the dried, use twice as many small fresh ginseng roots.*

**TIP:** *Cooked chestnuts are often sold in Asian markets in small vacuum-packed bags. Jarred cooked chestnuts are widely available and can be found online. For this recipe, you can also use raw chestnuts that you've roasted, boiled, or steamed yourself.*

# SEAWEED SOUP

## *MIYUK GUK*

**SERVES 4**

In Korea, this soup is offered to new mothers, especially those who are breastfeeding. Seaweed is rich in nutrients and is supposed to help the mother heal as well as make the baby strong. It's also commonly served at birthday celebrations as a nod back to the mother's postpartum diet.

Note that you can't substitute the roasted seaweed (*kim*) used elsewhere in the book for the dried sea mustard or brown seaweed (*miyuk*) called for here. *Miyuk* is available in whole sheets or in strips. I find the strips easier to work with, although sometimes they still need to be cut into smaller pieces before cooking. If you don't have a kitchen scale, the best way to get a measurement is to cram the cut strips into a measuring cup.

---

**1 ounce dried sea mustard or brown seaweed (*miyuk*), cut into bite-size pieces (about 2 packed cups)**

**8 ounces skirt steak or beef brisket, trimmed of fat and cut into bite-size strips**

**6 cloves garlic, grated or minced**

**1 tablespoon fish sauce**

**1 tablespoons soy sauce**

**3 teaspoons toasted sesame oil**

**1 teaspoon kosher salt or sea salt**

**8 cups starchy water (see Note)**

**Roasted sesame seeds (optional)**

**Steamed White Rice (page 106), for serving (see Note)**

SOAK THE SEAWEED in a large bowl of cold water for about 30 minutes. Rinse thoroughly 2 or 3 times and drain. The seaweed will swell considerably, so cut it again into bite-size pieces.

In a large bowl, toss together the beef, garlic, fish sauce, soy sauce, 2 teaspoons of the sesame oil, and the salt. Let marinate at room temperature for about 10 minutes.

In a large heavy-bottomed pot, heat the remaining 1 teaspoon sesame oil over medium-high heat. Add the beef mixture and cook, stirring often, until the meat loses most of its pinkness, about 1 minute. Add the drained seaweed and cook, stirring often, for a few minutes more.

Add the 8 cups water used to rinse the rice and bring to a boil over high heat. Skim off any scum or foam, and reduce the heat to maintain a simmer for about 30 minutes. Serve in bowls, sprinkled with sesame seeds, if desired, and with rice on the side. You can also put the rice into the soup, if you like.

---

TIP: *There are variations on this soup—some use clams and mussels to boost the briny flavor, some use chicken for a different flavor profile. Another variation uses Oxtail Soup (page 140) as the soup base and the shredded cooked oxtail as a substitute for the beef.*

NOTE: *Before cooking the rice, rinse it in 8 cups water and reserve the starchy rinsing water to make the soup.*

# OXTAIL SOUP

## *GORI GOMTANG*

**SERVES 4 TO 6**

If you're in the mood for a very comforting soup, try this. It's a tad time intensive, but very easy to make. I suggest you make it the day before you serve it, because like many soups, it tastes better with time. Another bonus is that the fat will float to the surface and solidify in a sheet while it's stored in the refrigerator; to remove it, all you have to do is lift it off. The soup is also the base for Rice Cake and Dumpling Soup (page 142).

**3½ to 4 pounds meaty oxtails, rinsed**

**4 cloves garlic, crushed**

**7 ounces Korean white radish (*mu*) or daikon, peeled, halved lengthwise, and cut crosswise into ¼-inch slices**

For Serving:

**Steamed White Rice (page 106)**

**Cabbage Kimchi (page 28)**

**Large handful of scallions, thinly sliced on an angle**

**Kosher salt or sea salt**

**Freshly ground black pepper**

PUT THE OXTAILS in a large pot and cover with very cold water. Let soak for 1 hour, draining and replacing the water every 20 minutes. (This helps to remove any excess blood.)

Rinse and drain the oxtails, cover with 8 cups cold water, and bring to a boil over high heat. Reduce the heat to a simmer until a lot of scum and foam rise to the water's surface, 5 to 10 minutes.

Transfer the oxtails to a large bowl, rinse well, and set aside. Discard the water from the pot and thoroughly wash the pot. Return the oxtails to the clean pot.

Add 18 cups water to the pot and bring to a boil over high heat. Reduce the heat to maintain a simmer for 2 hours, regularly skimming off any scum or fat that rises to the surface. If at any point the oxtails poke out from the liquid, add enough boiling water to cover. Add the garlic and continue simmering, skimming, and watching for bobbing oxtails until the liquid has reduced by about half (to 9 cups) and the meat is falling off the bones, about 30 minutes more. Discard the garlic and transfer the oxtails to a bowl; cover and keep warm. Skim off any remaining fat from the pot (some beads of fat are fine).

Add the radish to the pot and simmer until tender, about 10 minutes. Meanwhile, if you prefer to remove and shred the meat from the oxtails rather than serve as is with the bones, do so now. Divide the oxtails or just the shredded meat and radish among four to six bowls and top with the broth. Serve the soup with rice, kimchi, the scallions, and salt and pepper so your guests can season the soup to their liking.

TIP: *The initial boiling and rinsing of the oxtails reduces the amount of impurities and fat released into the broth, making it very clean looking. You can skip this process, but you'll need to do more skimming while the soup simmers.*

# MRS. KIM'S GOCHUJANG STEW

*MRS. KIM'S GOCHUJANG JJIGAE*

**SERVES 6**

This recipe is from the lovely owner of Los Angeles's famed Parks BBQ, Mrs. Jenee Kim. After my dear friend Craig Min introduced me to this chile-packed stew at the restaurant, I had to ask Mrs. Kim for the recipe.

1½ pounds skirt steak, beef brisket, or flank steak, trimmed of fat

1 tablespoon kosher salt or sea salt

10 cloves garlic, grated or minced

¼ cup *gochujang* (Korean chile paste)

2 teaspoons *gochugaru* (Korean chile flakes)

2 teaspoons freshly ground black pepper

¾ pound Yukon Gold potatoes, cut into ½-inch slices

1 onion, thinly sliced

7 ounces firm tofu, drained and cut into ¾-inch cubes

1 medium zucchini, halved lengthwise and cut into ½-inch slices

1 jalapeño, thinly sliced

Steamed White Rice (page 106), for serving

IN A MEDIUM heavy-bottomed saucepan, combine the beef, salt, and 6 cups water and bring to a boil over high heat. Reduce the heat to maintain a simmer, occasionally skimming off any scum that rises to the top, until the meat is very tender, 3 to 3½ hours.

Transfer the meat to a cutting board, cover with plastic wrap to keep it moist, and set aside. Pass the braising liquid through a fine-mesh strainer into another medium heavy-bottomed saucepan (or strain into a bowl and return the liquid to the same saucepan), discarding any solids.

Add the garlic, chile paste, chile flakes, and pepper, stir to combine, and bring to a boil over high heat. Reduce the heat to maintain a simmer for 20 minutes.

Add the potatoes and onion and cook until the potatoes are tender, about 20 minutes. Meanwhile, cut the meat crosswise into pieces about 2½ inches wide and then slice the meat against the grain into ¼-inch-wide strips. If the broth is very thin, mash some of the potatoes into it.

Return the meat to the pot. Add the tofu, zucchini, and jalapeño and simmer until the zucchini is tender, 6 to 8 minutes. Transfer to a serving bowl and serve with rice.

# RICE CAKE AND DUMPLING SOUP

*DDUK MANDU GUK*

**SERVES 4**

It is tradition in Korea to eat this soup for the Lunar New Year. I recommend using my Oxtail Soup (page 140) as the base, but for a quick version, store-bought chicken broth and frozen dumplings will do. You can also lose the dumplings and double the amount of rice cakes to make rice cake soup (*dduk guk*).

1 teaspoon vegetable oil

Kosher salt or sea salt

2 large eggs, lightly beaten with a splash of water

8 cups Oxtail Soup (page 140)

24 Meaty Dumplings (page 54)

½ cup meat picked from the oxtails from Oxtail Soup (page 140), shredded (optional)

8 ounces sliced rice cakes (*dduk*), soaked in cold water for 15 to 30 minutes and then drained

Freshly ground black pepper

Large handful of scallions, thinly sliced on an angle

Large handful of julienned roasted seaweed (*kim*)

Roasted sesame seeds

IN A MEDIUM nonstick skillet, heat the oil over medium heat. Beat a pinch of salt into the eggs and add them to the skillet, swirling to evenly coat the bottom. Cook, without touching, until the egg is set but just barely browned on the bottom, about 2 minutes. Flip and continue to cook until the bottom is set, again trying not to get too much color on the egg, 15 to 20 seconds more. Slide onto a cutting board, cut into thirds, and cut crosswise into thin strips. Set the egg strips aside.

In a large pot, bring the soup to a boil over high heat. Add the dumplings, stirring gently so they don't stick to one another, and simmer for 4 minutes (a little longer if the dumplings are frozen). Add the oxtail meat (if using) and rice cakes and continue to simmer until the dumplings are cooked through and the rice cakes are soft, about 2 minutes more. They should both float to the top of the soup. Season the soup with salt and pepper, but not too aggressively, as the dumplings have a lot of flavor.

Divide the soup, rice cakes, dumplings, and oxtail meat (if using) among four to six bowls. Top with the egg strips, scallions, seaweed, and sesame seeds and serve immediately.

TIP: *Instead of making an omelet, the eggs can also be drizzled into the pot of soup at the end of cooking to form ribbons of eggs, like egg drop soup.*

# PORK AND KIMCHI STEW

*KIMCHI JJIGAE*

**SERVES 4**

When your kimchi is getting a little funky smelling and fizzy, instead of throwing it out, make this tasty stew. Just be sure to turn the exhaust fan on high and maybe open a few windows, because the kimchi is known to fill the house with a strong smell! You'll be well rewarded with a healthful, umami-packed soup that is surprisingly soothing. This stew is a staple in Korean cuisine, and so satisfying with its heat and spice.

1 tablespoon vegetable oil

10 ounces skinless pork belly, cut crosswise into 2-inch pieces and then lengthwise into ¼-inch slices

2½ cups packed drained Cabbage Kimchi (page 28), coarsely chopped, plus ¼ cup kimchi liquid

3 tablespoons *gochujang* (Korean chile paste)

1 teaspoon sugar

Kosher salt or sea salt

14 ounces firm tofu, drained, cut lengthwise into ½-inch-thick slices, then halved crosswise

10 fresh Asian chives, cut into 1½-inch pieces

1 scallion, thinly sliced on an angle

1 small fresh Korean red chile or Fresno chile, thinly sliced (with seeds) on an angle

Toasted sesame oil, for serving

Steamed White Rice (page 106), for serving

IN A MEDIUM saucepan, heat the vegetable oil over medium heat. Add the pork and cook until some of the fat has rendered and the meat is mostly no longer pink, about 5 minutes. Raise the heat to medium-high, add the kimchi, kimchi liquid, chile paste, sugar, and a pinch of salt, and stir to combine. Add 3½ cups water and bring to a boil over high heat, stirring often. Reduce the heat to maintain a simmer for 15 minutes more.

Add the tofu and cook to heat through, 2 to 3 minutes. Stir in the chives, scallion, and chile. Transfer to a serving bowl, drizzle with sesame oil, and serve with rice.

# SEAFOOD

# STEAMED GINGER SEA BASS
## *WITH GINGER SAUCE*

**SERVES 4**

My head chef, Andy Hales, and I developed a similar dish together at the first restaurant where I served as executive chef in London. It's very healthy and delicately flavored, and when we took it off the menu, people complained so much that we had to put it back on—and left it on.

You can steam the fish in a bamboo or metal steamer basket set over a wok, saucepan, or skillet, or in a Western-style steamer set. I like to use a double-tiered steamer basket, but if you don't have one, it's preferable to use two steamer setups rather than cook the fish in batches, so the first batch doesn't get cold in the meantime.

Sauce:

**5 tablespoons soy sauce**

**3 tablespoons mirin**

**1 tablespoon sugar**

**1 (1½-inch) knob fresh ginger, peeled and finely julienned**

**2 teaspoons roasted sesame seeds**

**½ teaspoon grated or minced garlic**

**Large pinch of *gochugaru* (Korean chile flakes; optional)**

Fish:

**4 boneless sea bass or branzino fillets (about 4 ounces each)**

**4 tablespoons mirin**

**Kosher salt or sea salt**

**6 thick slices unpeeled fresh ginger (cut on an angle)**

**4 large cloves garlic, sliced lengthwise**

For Serving:

**Zucchini Ribbons (page 100; optional)**

**Small handful of finely chopped fresh chives**

**Black sesame seeds**

**Roasted sesame seeds**

**Dried chile threads (*silgochu*)**

**Steamed White Rice (page 106)**

FOR THE SAUCE: In a small saucepan, combine the soy sauce, mirin, and sugar and stir over medium-high heat until the sugar has dissolved. Stir in the ginger, sesame seeds, garlic, and chile flakes (if using) and set aside to infuse while the fish is steaming.

FOR THE FISH: Score each fillet crosswise five or six times as you gently squeeze the fillet lengthwise so that it puckers up. Be careful not to cut too deeply; you want to slice through the skin and just a bit of the flesh. Sprinkle both sides of each fillet with 1 tablespoon of the mirin and a little salt; set aside.

Fill the base of your steamer setup with 1 inch of water and bring to a steady simmer. Cut 2 rounds

of parchment paper just slightly smaller than the bottom of the steamer baskets. Cut small holes in the parchment (similar to the way you made paper snowflakes as a kid) for the steam to go through.

Lay the parchment in the bottom of the steamer baskets. Scatter the ginger and garlic on the parchment, then top with the fillets, skin-side up. Drizzle the fillets with the remaining 3 table-spoons mirin, set the baskets over the simmering water, cover, and steam until the flesh is opaque and flakes easily with a fork, about 8 minutes. Remove from the heat.

Mound the zucchini ribbons (if using) in the middle of four plates. Carefully place a fillet, skin-side up, on top of each mound. Sprinkle the fillets with the chives and both types of sesame seeds. Spoon about 1 tablespoon of the reserved sauce, including the ginger threads, over each fillet and garnish with chile threads. Serve with the rice and remaining sauce on the side.

# SIMPLY BROILED MACKEREL

*GODEUNGEO GUI*

**SERVES 4**

Not only is broiled mackerel a delicious and inexpensive dish, it's one of the easiest and fastest you can make: about five minutes from start to finish. I am always surprised with how good it tastes.

My mom used to serve this dish up as a simple dinner, or one fillet as part of the *banchan* on the table.

4 boneless blue mackerel fillets (about 5 ounces each), patted dry

Vegetable oil, for broiling

Kosher salt or sea salt

Steamed White Rice (page 106), for serving

Lemon wedges, for serving

PREHEAT THE BROILER and position a rack 4 to 5 inches from the heat source. Line a baking sheet with aluminum foil.

Score each fillet crosswise three or four times as you gently squeeze the top and bottom of the fillet together so that it puckers up. Be careful not to cut too deeply; you want to slice through the skin and just a bit of the flesh. This helps the fillets cook more evenly.

Lightly coat both sides of the fillets with oil, season with salt, and arrange skin-side up on the prepared baking sheet. Broil until the skin is lightly golden and blistered in spots and the flesh is cooked through, about 5 minutes. Serve on plates with rice and lemon wedges.

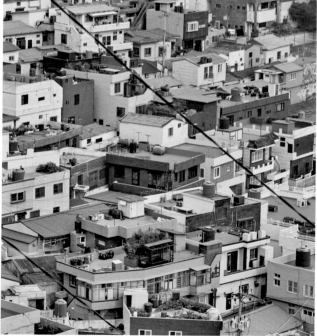

# FRIED FISH WITH KIMCHI MAYO
## *AND SESAME MUSHY PEAS*

**SERVES 4**

Having lived in London for about a decade now, it's not surprising that I've become a huge fan of fish and chips. I like to mix strong Korean flavors into the batter, but keep the crust nice and light and crispy. A good crust is key to good fried fish. Once you see how easy it is to fry your own, you won't need to go out for it anymore. As for the peas, never in a million years did I think I'd like mushy ones, as they're usually very bland, but their comforting quality slowly grew on me. I think you'll like my Korean twist on them. For authentic mushy peas, try to find the marrowfat variety (you'll have to soak them overnight with baking soda).

Kimchi Mayo:

½ cup mayonnaise, preferably Kewpie or a Korean brand

3 tablespoons finely chopped Cabbage Kimchi (page 28) with juices

Sesame Mushy Peas:

Kosher salt or sea salt

4 cups frozen peas

2 small cloves garlic

2 teaspoons toasted sesame oil

Freshly ground black pepper

Fish:

Vegetable oil, for frying

1⅓ cups tempura flour, plus more for sprinkling

2 tablespoons juice from Cabbage Kimchi (page 28)

1 tablespoon *gochujang* (Korean chile paste)

1 teaspoon garlic powder

1 teaspoon onion powder

1 cup plus 2 tablespoons seltzer water, well-chilled

4 (6-ounce) boneless skinless cod fillets, patted dry

Kosher salt or sea salt

Freshly ground black pepper

For Serving:

Flaky sea salt, such as Maldon (optional)

Pinch of *gochugaru* (Korean chile flakes; optional)

4 lemon wedges

FOR THE KIMCHI MAYO: In a small bowl, stir together the mayonnaise and kimchi. Cover the kimchi mayo and refrigerate.

FOR THE MUSHY PEAS: Bring a medium saucepan of salted water to a boil. Add the peas and boil until bright green and soft, 2 to 2½ minutes. Drain well and transfer to a food processor. Add the garlic and sesame oil and season with salt and a generous amount of pepper. Process until a chunky paste forms. Rinse out the saucepan, return the mushy peas to the pan, and keep warm.

FOR THE FISH: In a large, wide, heavy-bottomed pot at least 5 inches deep, heat 2 inches of oil over medium-high heat until it reaches 375°F. Meanwhile, in a large bowl, whisk together the flour, kimchi juice, chile paste, garlic powder, and onion powder into a thick paste. Whisk in the seltzer water, being careful not to overmix. A few lumps in the batter are okay.

Generously season the cod fillets with salt and pepper and then lightly sprinkle both sides with tempura flour. Spread with your fingers to coat evenly. Working in batches, dip each fillet into the batter, letting any excess drip off. Suspend the fillet in the oil for a couple of seconds to set the crust before letting it slip completely into the oil;

otherwise, it will stick to the bottom of the pot. Fry the fish, flipping halfway through, until golden brown and cooked through, about 3 minutes. Transfer to a wire rack or paper towel–lined plate to drain and immediately season with salt or flaky sea salt and chile flakes, if desired. Repeat with remaining fish, letting the oil come back to temperature before cooking the next batch.

Serve immediately, with the kimchi mayo, mushy peas, and lemon wedges.

TIP: *If you'd like to add some chips to your fish and mushy peas, coat some scrubbed and thinly sliced (about ¼-inch-thick) sweet potato rounds in the remaining batter. Fry in the oil until golden and cooked through. Drain, season with salt, and serve hot.*

# GOCHUJANG-GLAZED SALMON

### SERVES 4

If you're reluctant to cook fish because you think it'll stink up the house, this is the recipe for you. As long as you discard the foil right after broiling, there won't be any lingering odors. It's also perfect for a dinner party because it takes so little time (less than ten minutes total) and attention. The glaze is so tasty and will work with other types of fish as well.

Vegetable oil, for broiling

4 (5- to 6-ounce) boneless skinless salmon fillets, preferably center cut

Kosher salt or sea salt

Freshly ground black pepper

6 tablespoons Gochujang Glaze (page 214)

For Serving:

Handful of scallions, thinly sliced on an angle

Black sesame seeds

Dried chile threads (*silgochu*)

Steamed White Rice (page 106)

PREHEAT THE BROILER and position a rack 4 to 5 inches from the heat source. Line a baking sheet with aluminum foil and grease the foil.

Put the salmon on the prepared baking sheet, lightly brush with oil, and season with salt and pepper. Broil for about 2 minutes. (If you're using thinner tail pieces, which will cook faster, you can skip this initial broiling.)

Brush the salmon with the glaze and broil until cooked to the desired doneness, about 5 minutes for medium-rare. Transfer to a platter, top with scallions, sesame seeds, and chile threads, and serve with rice.

TIP: *If you happen to get skin-on salmon, don't bother removing the skin yourself. Just skip greasing the foil, put the salmon on it skin-side down, and lightly brush the top with oil. The skin should stick to the foil once cooked and the salmon can be lifted easily from it with a spatula.*

# FRIED SHRIMP WITH GARLICKY HOT PEPPER SAUCE

## *KKANPOONG SAEWOO*

**SERVES 4**

This classic Korean-Chinese dish is a more grown-up version of sweet-and-sour shrimp. The shrimp is battered and fried and then enrobed in a spicy, garlicky, pungent sauce, free of the distraction of vegetables. With its somewhat familiar tomato-accented sauce, it's more similar to Chinese sweet-and-sour takeout than its cousin, Sweet-and-Sour Beef (page 183).

1 teaspoon plus 1 tablespoon vegetable oil, plus more for frying

½ cup plus 1 teaspoon cornstarch

½ cup potato starch

½ teaspoon baking soda

Kosher salt or sea salt

1 large egg white

1½ pounds large shrimp, peeled, deveined, and patted dry

3 tablespoons sugar

4½ teaspoons tomato paste

1 tablespoon soy sauce

1 tablespoon rice vinegar

1 teaspoon *gochujang* (Korean chile paste), Sriracha, chile sauce, or chile-garlic sauce

1 teaspoon toasted sesame oil

3 tablespoons diced onion

6 cloves garlic, grated or minced

1 fresh Korean red chile or Fresno chile, diced

1 fresh Korean green chile or jalapeño, diced

Handful of scallions, thinly sliced on an angle

Steamed White Rice (page 106), for serving

IN A LARGE, wide, heavy-bottomed pot at least 5 inches deep, heat 2 inches of vegetable oil over medium-high heat until it reaches 375°F. While the oil is heating, in a large bowl, whisk together ½ cup of the cornstarch, the potato starch, baking soda, and a pinch of salt. Add the egg white, 1 teaspoon of the vegetable oil, and ½ cup water and whisk until a thick batter forms.

Working in batches, coat the shrimp in the batter, letting any excess drip into the bowl. Slip the shrimp into the oil, one piece at a time, and fry, stirring occasionally, until golden brown, about 1½ minutes. Transfer to a wire rack or paper towel–lined plate to drain. Repeat with the remaining shrimp, letting the oil return to 375°F between batches.

When all the shrimp have been fried, let the oil return to 375°F, and then carefully return all the shrimp to the oil and fry a second time until very crisp, 1½ to 2 minutes. Transfer to a wire rack or paper towel–lined plate to drain. Set the fried shrimp aside.

In a small bowl, whisk together the sugar, tomato paste, soy sauce, vinegar, chile paste, sesame oil, remaining 1 teaspoon cornstarch, and ¼ cup water until the sugar has dissolved. Set the sauce mixture aside.

In a large skillet, heat the remaining 1 tablespoon vegetable oil over medium-high heat. Add the onion, garlic, and red and green chiles and cook, stirring, until just fragrant, about 30 seconds. Add the sauce mixture and cook, stirring, until the sauce thickens and becomes glossy, about 45 seconds. Add the fried shrimp, toss quickly to coat, and transfer to a platter. Scatter the scallions over the top and serve immediately with rice.

# SPICY SQUID STIR-FRY

## *OJINGUH BOKKEUM*

**SERVES 4**

Be sure to use fresh squid for this recipe, as it does make a big difference. I love eating this dish for lunch with a side of rice. It cooks in no time at all and is so popular with my friends.

5 cloves garlic, grated or minced

2 tablespoons *gochujang* (Korean chile paste)

2 tablespoons soy sauce

1 tablespoon sesame oil

1 tablespoon *gochugaru* (Korean chile flakes)

4½ teaspoons sugar

1 pound squid, bodies and tentacles separated, rinsed, and patted dry

1 tablespoon vegetable oil

2 small carrots, thinly sliced

1 onion, thinly sliced

4 scallions, whites and greens separated and cut into 1½-inch pieces

1 small fresh Korean red chile or Fresno chile, thinly sliced on an angle

Roasted sesame seeds, for serving

Steamed White Rice (page 106), for serving

IN A MEDIUM BOWL, stir together the garlic, chile paste, soy sauce, sesame oil, chile flakes, and sugar. Set the sauce aside.

Cut the squid bodies open, lay them flat, and score one side in a crosshatch pattern, being careful not to cut all the way through the flesh. Cut the bodies lengthwise into 1-inch-wide strips. Cut any large tentacles in half. Add the squid to the sauce and toss to coat. Let marinate at room temperature for 10 to 15 minutes.

In a large skillet, heat the vegetable oil over medium-high heat. Add the carrots, onion, and scallion whites and cook, stirring often, until the carrots are crisp-tender, about 2 minutes. Add the squid and sauce and cook, stirring often, until the squid is tender and just cooked through, 2 to 3 minutes. Do not overcook or the squid will become tough. Stir in the scallion greens and chile and remove from the heat.

Transfer to a platter, sprinkle with sesame seeds, and serve with rice.

# SPICY MUSSELS WITH BACON

**SERVES 2**

I crave eating mussels in the true Belgium style—a big, indulgent pot teeming with juicy morsels from the sea. Here, I borrow from that wonderful tradition and add some Korean flavors. Serve the mussels with steamed white rice, which is great for soaking up the broth left at the bottom of the bowl.

1 tablespoon vegetable oil

4 slices thick-cut bacon, cut crosswise into ½-inch pieces

2 large cloves garlic, grated or minced

1 large shallot, thinly sliced into rings

½ cup dry vermouth or white wine

½ cup chicken stock

3 tablespoons mirin

1 tablespoon *doenjang* (Korean soybean paste)

1 teaspoon *gochujang* (Korean chile paste)

1 fresh Korean red chile or Fresno chile, thinly sliced on an angle

2 pounds mussels, cleaned and debearded

Handful of fresh chives, cut into ½-inch pieces, for serving

Steamed White Rice (page 106), for serving

Lemon wedges or halves, for serving

IN A MEDIUM, wide, heavy-bottomed pot, heat the oil over medium heat. Add the bacon and cook, stirring occasionally, until the edges just start to brown, 3 to 4 minutes. Add the garlic and shallot and cook, stirring occasionally, until softened, another minute or two. Add the vermouth, raise the heat to high, and bring to a boil. Add the stock and mirin and then whisk in the soybean paste and chile paste until they have dissolved.

Stir in the chile and then the mussels. Cover the pot and cook, shaking occasionally to redistribute the ingredients, until the mussels open, about 3 minutes. Discard any mussels that don't open. Spoon the mussels and broth into bowls, scatter the chives on top, and serve with rice and lemons.

CHICKEN

# ULTIMATE KFC (KOREAN FRIED CHICKEN)

*YANGNYUM CHICKEN*

**SERVES 4**

I have always loved fried chicken. But even though I grew up eating it in America, for me, "KFC" stands for Korean fried chicken. There are many different versions, but what they all have in common is a very thin, hard crisp coating, which comes from using cornstarch instead of flour, as well as double frying. My take on the dish, which includes vodka and matzo meal, is a little unorthodox and has a fair number of ingredients, but I call it "ultimate" for a reason. Two things make it even better: its customary accompaniment of Cubed Pickled Radish (page 34) and ice-cold beer.

## Coating:

¼ cup cornstarch

2½ teaspoons kosher salt or sea salt

½ teaspoon baking powder

Freshly ground black pepper

2 chicken drumsticks, 2 thighs, and 4 wings (with tips)

## BBQ Sauce:

3 tablespoons Korean chile paste (*gochujang*)

3 tablespoons ketchup

2 tablespoons packed dark brown sugar

2 tablespoons soy sauce

1 tablespoon toasted sesame oil

2 teaspoons grated peeled fresh ginger

2 cloves garlic, grated or minced

Vegetable oil, for frying

## Batter:

½ cup cornstarch

¼ cup fine matzo meal

¼ cup all-purpose flour

2 tablespoons *gochugaru* (Korean chile flakes)

1 tablespoon kosher salt or sea salt

2½ teaspoons garlic powder

2½ teaspoons onion powder

¼ teaspoon baking powder

⅓ cup vodka (or any neutral-tasting 40 proof alcohol)

2 tablespoons *gochujang* (Korean chile paste)

FOR THE COATING: In a large bowl, stir together the cornstarch, salt, baking powder, and a generous amount of pepper.

Add the chicken and toss to coat. Transfer the chicken to a wire rack, shaking each piece to remove any excess coating. Let sit, uncovered, at room temperature for about 1 hour.

FOR THE BBQ SAUCE: Meanwhile, in a small saucepan, combine all the sauce ingredients and simmer until slightly thickened, 3 to 5 minutes. The sauce can be either served with the chicken or drizzled over it. If you prefer the latter, remove it from the heat on the early side so it's a little thinner. Set aside; the sauce is best warm or at room temperature.

Shortly before cooking, in a large, wide, heavy-bottomed pot at least 5 inches deep, heat 2 inches of vegetable oil over medium-high heat until it reaches 350°F.

FOR THE BATTER: While the oil is heating, in a large bowl, whisk together the cornstarch, matzo meal, flour, chile flakes, salt, garlic powder, onion powder, and baking powder. In a small bowl, whisk together the vodka, chile paste, and 1 cup water.

Right before you're ready to fry the chicken, whisk the vodka mixture into the cornstarch mixture. (Don't do this in advance or the resulting batter may thicken too much as it sits. The consistency should be relatively thin and runny.)

Working in two batches, with the legs and thighs together as one batch and the wings as the other, dip each piece of chicken into the batter, letting any excess drip off. Suspend the chicken in the oil for a couple of seconds to set the crust before letting it slip completely into the oil; otherwise, it will stick to the bottom of the pot. Fry the chicken, flipping halfway through, until golden brown and cooked through, 15 to 20 minutes. Transfer to a wire rack or paper towel–lined plate to drain. Let the oil return to 350°F before cooking the second batch.

Serve the chicken with the BBQ sauce either drizzled on top or on the side.

TIP: *Boneless skinless thighs fried this way make an awesome sandwich. Serve the chicken on rolls slathered with the BBQ sauce and topped with iceberg lettuce and Spicy Pickled Radish Salad (page 34).*

# CHICKEN SKEWERS

*DAK GGOCHI*

**SERVES 4**

The Korean street scene is full of food served on sticks. This street food–inspired dish is easy to make, very flavorful, and great for groups large and small. (It's fun to let people assemble their own, too.) I also like to wrap the chicken and spiced mayo in lettuce leaves or tortillas with Steamed White Rice (page 106).

2 tablespoons mirin

1 tablespoon soy sauce

1 tablespoon toasted sesame oil

1 large clove garlic, grated or minced

8 ounces boneless skinless chicken thighs, cut crosswise into a total of twelve ¾-inch-wide pieces

3 tablespoons mayonnaise, preferably Kewpie or a Korean brand

2 to 2½ tablespoons Spicy Lettuce Wrap Sauce (page 213)

12 carrot sticks, 3-inch long x ½-inch wide

4 scallions, cut into 3-inch-long pieces

6 large shiitake mushrooms, stemmed and halved

Vegetable oil, for grilling

Kosher salt or sea salt

Handful of scallions, thinly sliced on an angle, for serving

IN A MEDIUM BOWL, combine the mirin, soy sauce, sesame oil, and garlic. Add the chicken and toss to coat. Cover and let marinate in the refrigerator, tossing once or twice, for at least 1 hour or up to overnight. Before grilling, let the chicken come to room temperature, about 30 minutes.

If using bamboo skewers, soak ten 10-inch-long skewers in water for at least an hour. (You'll only need eight skewers, but we're allowing for possible breakage.) Alternatively, use eight metal skewers.

In a small bowl, stir together the mayonnaise and lettuce wrap sauce (start with 2 tablespoons and add more to taste). Cover the spicy lettuce wrap sauce mayonnaise and refrigerate.

Preheat a gas or charcoal grill to medium.

Meanwhile, bring a small saucepan of water to a boil over high heat. Blanch the carrots until just barely softened, about 45 to 60 seconds. Drain, rinse under cold water to cool, drain again, and pat dry.

Using two skewers parallel to each other, form a ladder by skewering the ingredients through both skewers in the following order a total of three times, leaving about a 1-inch-wide space between the skewers: scallion, marinated chicken, blanched carrot, shiitake. Allow a little space between each ingredient for even cooking. Repeat with the remaining skewers, vegetables, and chicken, ending up with a total of four sets of skewers. Lightly brush the vegetables and chicken with vegetable oil and season with salt.

Arrange the skewers on the grill without crowding. Grill, covered, until the vegetables and chicken are charred in spots and cooked through, 5 to 6 minutes total, flipping halfway through. Transfer the skewers to a platter. If using metal skewers, carefully remove the vegetables and chicken before serving because the metal will be too hot to handle with bare hands. Sprinkle with the sliced scallions and serve with the spicy lettuce wrap sauce mayonnaise.

TIP: *For a pretty presentation, cut several scallions lengthwise into thin strips and put in a bowl of ice water until they curl. Drain and use as a bed for the grilled skewers.*

# BRAISED CHICKEN WITH VEGETABLES

*JJIM DAK*

**SERVES 4**

While this hearty dish originated from the traditional town of Andong in Korea, it's now served in restaurants throughout the country and there are even restaurant franchises that specialize in it. It's spicy, but if you want less heat, remove the seeds from the chiles. Many versions use bone-in chicken, but I like the ease of boneless.

Sauce:

¼ cup soy sauce

5 cloves garlic, grated or minced

3 tablespoons oyster sauce

2 tablespoons sake

1 tablespoon dark brown sugar

1 tablespoon honey

1 teaspoon grated peeled fresh ginger

Chicken:

3 tablespoons vegetable oil

5 dried chiles, stems removed

2 pounds boneless skinless chicken thighs, halved crosswise

Kosher salt or sea salt

Freshly ground black pepper

1 onion, thinly sliced

8 ounces new potatoes (a mix of red, purple, and golden, if possible), peeled and halved

12 large shiitake mushrooms, stemmed and halved

3 carrots, cut on an angle into ¾-inch slices

6 scallions, cut into 2-inch pieces, whites and greens separated

4 ounces sweet potato noodles (*dangmyun*), soaked in warm water for about 20 minutes and then drained

2 fresh Korean red chiles or Fresno chiles, thinly sliced

2 fresh Korean green chiles or jalapeños, thinly sliced

For Serving:

Toasted sesame oil

Roasted sesame seeds

1 (3½-ounce) package enoki mushrooms, roots trimmed (optional)

Steamed White Rice (page 106)

FOR THE SAUCE: In a small bowl, stir together all the sauce ingredients and 1½ cups water. Set aside.

FOR THE CHICKEN: In a large, wide, heavy-bottomed pot, heat the oil over medium-high heat. Add the dried chiles and toast, stirring, until fragrant, about 10 seconds. Transfer to a plate and set aside. Working in batches if needed, add the chicken to the pot, season generously with salt and pepper, and cook, stirring occasionally, until lightly browned all over, 6 to 8 minutes. Transfer to a medium bowl and set aside. Repeat with the remaining chicken.

Add the onion and potatoes to the pot and cook, stirring occasionally, for about 1 minute. Add the sauce, toasted dried chiles, and chicken and any juices that have accumulated in the bowl, stir, and bring to a boil over high heat. Reduce the heat to maintain a simmer, covered, for about 10 minutes. Add the mushrooms, carrots, and scallion whites and simmer, stirring occasionally, until the carrots have softened, about 10 minutes more.

Add the noodles, scallion greens, and red and green chiles to the pot and cook, tossing occasionally, until the noodles become translucent and the sauce thickens slightly, about 5 minutes.

Drizzle with sesame oil, scatter with sesame seeds and the enoki mushrooms, if desired, and serve immediately (the noodles will continue to soak up liquid as it sits) in bowls with rice.

TIP: *There are many variations on this dish, so feel free to make your own. If you'd like more green vegetables, stir in some spinach when you add the noodles. If you'd like more sweetness, substitute some Korean sweet potatoes for the new potatoes.*

# MOM'S BBQ CHICKEN

## *UMMA'S DAK GOGI*

**SERVES 4**

My mom's BBQ chicken is the stuff of legend. She even used to grill it in our garage in unfavorable weather. I remember sitting on the steps staring at the little grill, watching her flip pieces of the juicy ginger-and-sesame-marinated chicken with chopsticks, and smelling the sweet smoke. Even your Korean-food-doubter friends will gladly chow down on this. To round out the dish, serve it with Grilled Corn on the Cob with Doenjang Butter (page 101) and Roasted Korean Sweet Potatoes (page 98) that you've peeled, mashed, and sprinkled with black sesame seeds, if you like.

1¼ cups soy sauce

½ cup packed dark brown sugar

6 scallions, thinly sliced on an angle

3 tablespoons rice vinegar

3 tablespoons maple syrup

2 tablespoons *gochujang* (Korean chile paste)

2 tablespoons toasted sesame oil

2 tablespoons grated peeled fresh ginger

2 tablespoons roasted sesame seeds

6 cloves garlic, grated or minced

Pinch of kosher salt or sea salt

Freshly ground black pepper

8 boneless skinless chicken thighs

Vegetable oil, for grilling

Doenjang Mayonnaise (page 216), for serving

IN A MEDIUM BOWL, stir together the soy sauce, brown sugar, scallions, vinegar, maple syrup, chile paste, sesame oil, ginger, sesame seeds, garlic, salt, and a generous amount of pepper until the sugar has dissolved. Transfer 1 cup of the marinade to a container, cover, and refrigerate. Add the chicken to the bowl with the remaining marinade and toss to coat. Cover and let marinate in the refrigerator, tossing once or twice, for at least 4 hours or up to overnight.

Before grilling, let the chicken come to room temperature, about 30 minutes. Meanwhile, put the reserved 1 cup marinade in a small saucepan and simmer until it has thickened to a glaze-like consistency, 8 to 10 minutes; set the glaze aside.

Preheat a gas or charcoal grill to medium-high heat.

Lightly brush the grates with vegetable oil. Shake any excess marinade off the chicken and arrange on the grill without crowding. Grill, flipping the thighs halfway through, until cooked through, about 15 minutes. Keep an eye on the temperature; if the grill is too hot, the outside of the thighs will burn before the inside is done. Transfer the chicken to a platter and brush very lightly with the glaze. The glaze can also be served on the side as a dipping sauce, along with the Doenjang Mayonnaise.

**TIP:** *If you prefer boneless skin-on chicken thighs and can't find them in the grocery, ask your butcher to debone skin-on thighs or simply use bone-in ones and just add a few minutes to the cooking time.*

BEEF &
LAMB

# THINLY SLICED BEEF WITH RICE CAKES

## *GOONG JOONG DDUKBOKKI*

**SERVES 4**

*Bulgogi* is one of the most popular and well-known Korean dishes; a royal version is to add rice cakes to it. The chewy rice cakes soak up the sweet sauce and add great texture. This dish is usually made with cylindrical-shaped *dduk*, but I like the sliced version here as I want the beef to be the star.

1 pound very thinly sliced beef *bulgogi* meat (sold at Korean markets) or rib eye

1 small unpeeled firm but ripe pear, grated (optional)

3 tablespoons sugar

3 tablespoons soy sauce

2 tablespoons roasted sesame oil

2 tablespoons vegetable oil

5 cloves garlic, grated or minced

2 tablespoons crushed roasted sesame seeds

1¼ teaspoons grated peeled fresh ginger

10 ounces sliced rice cakes (*dduk*)

1 small onion, thinly sliced

4 button mushrooms, sliced

1 small carrot, julienned

2 fresh garlic chives (optional), cut into 3-inch pieces, for serving

Black sesame seeds, for serving

Roasted sesame seeds, for serving

IN A SHALLOW DISH, combine the beef, pear (if using), and sugar and massage with your hands to thoroughly combine. Let sit for about 30 minutes at room temperature. Meanwhile, in a large bowl, stir together the soy sauce, sesame oil, 1 tablespoon of the vegetable oil, the garlic, crushed sesame seeds, and ginger; set the marinade aside.

When the beef is ready, use your hands to shake off and squeeze out any excess sugary liquid and then add the beef to the marinade. Toss to coat, cover, and let marinate for about 30 minutes at room temperature, or up to overnight in the refrigerator.

About 30 minutes before cooking, soak the rice cakes in a large bowl with enough water to cover.

When the rice cakes are ready, in a large skillet, heat the remaining 1 tablespoon vegetable oil over medium heat. Add the onion and cook until softened, 6 to 8 minutes. Add the mushrooms and carrot and cook until slightly softened, 5 minutes more. Raise the heat to medium-high, add the marinated beef, including the marinade, and cook, stirring occasionally, until the meat is still slightly pink, 2 to 3 minutes.

Grab the rice cakes from the bowl in handfuls, giving them a shake to drain, and add them to the skillet along with about ¼ cup of the soaking water, which will help create and thicken the sauce. Stir well and cook until the rice cakes are pliable and heated through, 2 to 3 minutes. Watch the rice cakes carefully because they get soft and mushy when overcooked. Transfer the mixture to a platter and sprinkle with the garlic chives and black and roasted sesame seeds.

TIP: *My favorite method for julienning carrots is to use a julienne peeler. Run the peeler down the entire carrot to get long strips and then cut crosswise as needed.*

# BRAISED BEEF SHORT RIBS

## *GALBI JJIM*

**SERVES 4 TO 6**

This dish hugs you back with its deep flavors. It is fantastic in the winter, when all you want is a hot stew to warm you from the inside out. I've simplified the method here to make it a one-pot, dump-it-all-in type of dish, but without sacrificing any flavor.

Kosher salt or sea salt

3 pounds beef short ribs, cut into 2-inch-long pieces (see Tip)

Vegetable oil

⅓ cup sake

1 large onion, halved and sliced

8 large cloves garlic, thinly sliced

3 tablespoons grated peeled fresh ginger

1 cup apple or pear juice

½ cup mirin

½ cup soy sauce

3 tablespoons brown sugar

3 tablespoons toasted sesame oil

2 teaspoons freshly ground black pepper

15 shiitake mushrooms, stemmed and halved

½ pound small new potatoes, halved

2 carrots, cut into 2-inch pieces

10 ounces Korean white radish (*mu*) or daikon, peeled and cut into ¾-inch pieces

For Serving:

1 (3½-ounce) package enoki mushrooms, roots trimmed

1 scallion, julienned or shredded (see Tip, page 90), put in a bowl of ice water until they curl and then drained

Large handful of pine nuts, toasted

Steamed White Rice (page 106)

GENEROUSLY SALT the ribs. In a large, wide, heavy-bottomed pot, heat 2 tablespoons of vegetable oil over medium-high heat. Working in batches, brown the ribs on all sides, about 8 minutes per batch. Transfer the ribs to a plate and repeat with the remaining ribs, adding more oil to the pot as needed. After the last batch, discard the oil in the pot. Add the sake and simmer, scraping up any browned bits on the bottom of the pot. Add the onion, garlic, and ginger and cook, stirring continuously, until just softened but not browned, about 2 minutes.

Stir in the apple juice, mirin, soy sauce, sugar, sesame oil, pepper, and salt to taste. Return the ribs and any juices that have accumulated on the plate to the pot. Add enough water to just barely cover the meat (about 2 cups) and bring to a boil over high heat. Reduce the heat to maintain a simmer, stirring occasionally, until the meat is very tender, about 2 hours.

Skim off any oil from the surface and then add the shiitakes, potatoes, carrots, and radish. Cover the

pot and continue to simmer until the vegetables are tender and the meat is falling off the bones, 45 minutes to 1 hour more.

Serve the ribs, vegetables, and broth in bowls, topped with the enoki mushrooms, scallion curls, and pine nuts and with the rice on the side.

TIP: *Ribs of this size are generally available at Korean markets; they still need to be cut apart lengthwise to separate the rib.*

# SWEET-AND-SOUR BEEF

## *TANGSUYUK*

**SERVES 4**

There are a handful of well-known Korean-Chinese dishes, and *tangsuyuk*, which can be made with beef, pork, or chicken, is one of the most popular. Note that although this is a quick dish to assemble once all the parts are in place, the starch mixture does require a three-hour or so resting period and the meat is fried twice to achieve extra-crispy results. The dipping sauce may also seem extraneous, but trust me, it makes the beef taste even better!

---

5 tablespoons soy sauce

6 tablespoons rice vinegar

1 cup plus 2 tablespoons potato starch

4 teaspoons vegetable oil, plus more for frying

1 small carrot, thinly sliced

½ small onion, cut into ½-inch squares

½ medium green bell pepper, cut into ½-inch squares

½ medium red bell pepper, cut into ½-inch squares

¾ cup ¾-inch-dice pineapple

Kosher salt or sea salt

6 tablespoons sugar

2 large egg whites

1¼ pounds sirloin or rib eye (½ inch thick), cut into strips about 3 inches long and 1 inch wide

Freshly ground black pepper

Steamed White Rice (page 106), for serving

IN A SMALL BOWL, stir together 2 tablespoons of the soy sauce and 1 tablespoon of the vinegar. Set the dipping sauce aside.

In a large bowl, whisk together 1 cup of the potato starch and 1 cup water. Refrigerate for 2½ to 3 hours. By the end of this period, the starch will have settled and solidified at the bottom of the bowl. Carefully pour out the water sitting on top, reserving the starch. Set the starch aside.

In a large nonstick skillet, heat 1 teaspoon of the oil over medium-high heat. Add the carrot and onion and cook, stirring often, for about 1 minute. Add the bell peppers and pineapple, season with salt, and cook, stirring often, for 1 minute more. Add the sugar, remaining 3 tablespoons soy sauce, remaining 5 tablespoons vinegar, and 1 cup water and cook, stirring often, until the sugar has dissolved. Remove from the heat and set the sauce mixture aside.

In a large, wide, heavy-bottomed pot at least 5 inches deep, heat 2 inches of oil over medium-high heat until it reaches 375°F. Meanwhile, add the egg whites and remaining 1 tablespoon oil to the bowl of starch and, using your fingers, stir until a batter forms. Season the beef with salt and pepper, add to the batter, and toss to coat.

Working in small batches, suspend each piece of beef in the oil for a couple of seconds to set the crust before letting it slip completely into the oil; otherwise, it will stick to the bottom of the pot. Fry, stirring often so the pieces don't stick together, until crisp, about 1½ minutes. Transfer to a wire rack or paper towel–lined plate to drain. Repeat with the remaining beef, letting the oil return to 375°F between batches.

When all the beef has been fried, let the oil return to 375°F, and then carefully return all the beef to the oil and fry a second time until very crisp, 1½ to 2 minutes. Transfer to a wire rack or paper towel–lined plate to drain. Season with salt and transfer the beef to a platter.

Reheat the sauce mixture over medium-high heat. In a cup, stir together the remaining 2 tablespoons potato starch and 2 tablespoons water to create a slurry. When the sauce mixture is hot, stir in the slurry, stirring continuously. As soon as the sauce has thickened, pour it over the beef on the platter and serve immediately with the rice and reserved dipping sauce.

# KRAZY KOREAN BURGERS

**SERVES 4**

It may seem crazy to fix it when it ain't broken, but I've Koreanized burgers and thrown in some pancetta to boot. Since pancetta is pork belly and a beloved cut in Korea, it just seemed to make sense. To me, at least. Sometimes you have to take these risks to come up with something phenomenal.

Pancetta can vary greatly in saltiness. If your pancetta isn't very salty, sprinkle some extra salt on the patties before cooking. Like most burgers, this one is good with chips, but instead of the typical potato variety, try Lotus Root Chips (page 58).

3 small cloves garlic

1 (½-inch) knob fresh ginger, peeled

4 ounces thinly sliced pancetta, coarsely chopped and kept cold

½ small white onion, coarsely chopped

1 tablespoon *gochugaru* (Korean chile flakes)

4 teaspoons *doenjang* (Korean soybean paste)

4 teaspoons *gochujang* (Korean chile paste)

2 teaspoons sugar

½ teaspoon freshly ground black pepper

1½ pounds ground beef chuck

2 tablespoons seltzer water, chilled

1 teaspoon roasted sesame seeds

1 tablespoon vegetable oil

Kosher salt or sea salt (optional)

For Serving:

4 large brioche buns, preferably topped with sesame seeds, split

2 tablespoons butter, softened

Red or green lettuce leaves

Cucumber Kimchi (page 36), sliced

Korean Ketchup (page 216)

¼ cup Doenjang Mayonnaise (page 216)

WITH THE MOTOR RUNNING, drop the garlic and ginger into a food processor and process until finely chopped. Add the pancetta and pulse until finely chopped. Add the onion, chile flakes, soybean paste, chile paste, sugar, and pepper and process until fairly smooth. Set the pancetta mixture aside.

Crumble the beef into a large bowl. Add the seltzer, sesame seeds, and pancetta mixture and gently mix together with your hands, being careful not to overwork the mixture. Form the mixture into four patties, each about 1 inch thick and 4 inches wide. Create a depression in the center of each patty, as burgers tend to rise in the middle during cooking and this will help the burgers come out flat. If not cooking immediately, cover the patties and refrigerate.

In a large skillet, heat the oil over medium-high heat. Lightly season the burgers with salt, if necessary. Put them in the skillet depression-side up and cook, flipping halfway through, until browned and cooked through, about 7 minutes.

Beef & Lamb

Meanwhile, heat a two-burner griddle/grill pan or skillet over medium-high heat. Spread both sides of the buns with the butter and cook cut-side down until lightly toasted, about a minute. If working in batches, toast the bottom buns first. Transfer to individual plates.

Put a burger on each bottom bun and top with lettuce and then the cucumber kimchi. Smear some Korean ketchup and *doenjang* mayonnaise on the top buns and place on the burgers. Secure with a bamboo skewer or long toothpick, if you like, and serve immediately.

# BBQ BEEF SHORT RIBS

*GALBI*

**SERVES 2**

*Galbi* is the ultimate classic in Korean BBQ. If someone is trying Korean food for the first time, this is the dish to start with. The ingredients are relatively easy to find, it's simple to make, and your guests will swoon in gastronomic delight. This recipe can easily be scaled up.

**1 Asian or 2 firm but ripe pears, peeled and grated**

**3½ tablespoons dark brown sugar**

**3 tablespoons soy sauce**

**2½ tablespoons toasted sesame oil**

**3 cloves garlic, grated or minced**

**2 teaspoons grated peeled fresh ginger**

**Large pinch of kosher salt or sea salt**

**Freshly ground black pepper**

**1 pound bone-in L.A.-cut beef short ribs (or trimmed boneless rib-eye steak, partially frozen and cut into ¼-inch-wide pieces)**

**Vegetable oil, for grilling**

For Serving:

**Red or green lettuce leaves**

**Perilla leaves (*ggaennip*), also known as sesame leaves (optional)**

**Steamed White Rice (page 106)**

**½ recipe Spicy Lettuce Wrap Sauce (page 213)**

**Spicy Scallion and Red Onion Salad (page 90)**

IN A MEDIUM BOWL, stir together the pears, sugar, soy sauce, sesame oil, garlic, ginger, salt, and pepper to taste until the sugar has dissolved. Add the beef and massage the marinade into the meat. Cover and let marinate in the refrigerator, tossing once or twice, for at least 2 hours or up to overnight. The longer you marinate the beef, the better it will taste.

Preheat a gas or charcoal grill until very hot.

Lightly brush the grates with vegetable oil. Shake any excess marinade off the beef and arrange the beef on the grill without crowding. Grill for about 30 seconds per side for rare, or longer, if you like. If you're using short ribs, cut the meat off the bones with kitchen shears. Transfer the meat to a platter and serve with the lettuce, perilla leaves (if using), rice, and spicy lettuce wrap sauce on the side. To assemble, put a lettuce leaf in one hand and top with a perilla leaf (if using), a spoonful of rice, a smear of sauce, a piece of beef, and some spicy scallion and red onion salad. Wrap the lettuce around the ingredients and enjoy.

# GRILLED HANGER STEAK

**SERVES 4**

I like to marinate hanger steak in a potent soy-and–sesame oil marinade that works in just fifteen minutes. The steak goes great with Kimchi-Apple Slaw (page 90). This is a relatively inexpensive cut of beef, but it is still full of rich flavor.

3 tablespoons sugar

6 tablespoons soy sauce

2 tablespoons vegetable oil, plus more for grilling

2 tablespoons toasted sesame oil

1 tablespoon grated peeled fresh ginger

3 cloves garlic, grated or minced

1 shallot, minced

Kosher salt or sea salt

Freshly ground black pepper

2 pounds hanger steak

Handful of thinly sliced scallions, for serving

Roasted sesame seeds, for serving

IN A LARGE BOWL, stir together the sugar, soy sauce, vegetable oil, sesame oil, ginger, garlic, shallots, and salt and pepper to taste until the sugar has dissolved. Add the steak, massage the marinade into the meat, and let sit at room temperature for 15 minutes.

Preheat a gas or charcoal grill until medium-hot.

Lightly brush the grates with vegetable oil. Grill the steak, flipping halfway through, until cooked to your liking, about 9 minutes total for medium-rare. Transfer to a cutting board and let rest for about 5 minutes. Thinly slice the steak against the grain, transfer to a platter, and top with the scallions and sesame seeds.

# SWEET-AND-SPICY GRILLED LAMB CHOPS

**SERVES 4**

Koreans do not eat a lot of lamb, but I think the flavors of Korea meld well with this meat. These chops go great with Grilled Twist Peppers (page 101) and Steamed White Rice (page 106).

¼ cup sake

¼ cup *gochujang* (Korean chile paste)

1 tablespoon *doenjang* (Korean soybean paste)

2 tablespoons mirin

1 tablespoon soy sauce

1 tablespoon toasted sesame oil

1½ teaspoons *gochugaru* (Korean chile flakes)

1 tablespoon honey

16 Frenched lamb rib chops
(about 3 ounces each)

Vegetable oil, for grilling

Roasted sesame seeds, for serving

IN A LARGE BOWL, whisk together the sake, chile paste, soybean paste, mirin, soy sauce, sesame oil, chile flakes, and honey until smooth. Add the lamb chops and toss to coat. Cover and let marinate in the refrigerator, tossing once or twice, for at least 4 hours or up to overnight. Before grilling, let the lamb chops come to room temperature, about 30 minutes.

Preheat a gas or charcoal grill to medium-hot.

Lightly brush the grates with vegetable oil. Cut a long strip of aluminum foil twice the length of the lamb chop bones, fold it in half, and lay it on the grill. Arrange the chops on the grill without crowding and with the bones over the foil so they don't burn. Grill, covered, flipping the chops halfway through, until cooked to your liking, about 7 minutes total for medium-rare. Transfer to a platter, sprinkle with sesame seeds, and let rest for about 5 minutes before serving.

# DOENJANG-GLAZED LAMB LETTUCE WRAPS

## *YANG GOGI SSAM*

**SERVES 6 TO 8**

Lamb is not very readily available in Korea, and it's been slow to gain an audience. I find, however, that it pairs really well with our strong flavors, like the *doenjang* glaze I use to marinate this boneless butterflied leg of lamb. Once the meat is marinated, the cooking is just a quick broil. So little work to feed a large group.

1 recipe Doenjang Glaze (page 216)

1 (3- to 3½-pound) butterflied boneless leg of lamb, with just a very thin cap of fat

Vegetable oil, for broiling

For Serving:

Handful of thinly sliced scallions

Small handful of roasted sesame seeds

Red or green lettuce leaves

Perilla leaves (*ggaennip*), also known as sesame leaves (optional)

Steamed White Rice (page 106)

Lettuce Wrap Sauce (page 213)

Spicy Pickled Radish Salad (page 34)

TRANSFER ¼ CUP of the glaze to a small container, cover, and refrigerate. Score the fat on the lamb. Put the lamb in a large bowl, add the remaining 1 cup glaze, and rub the glaze all over the meat. Cover and let marinate in the refrigerator, tossing once or twice, for at least 8 hours or up to 24 hours. Before broiling, let the lamb come to room temperature, about 1 hour.

Preheat the broiler and position a rack 4 to 5 inches from the heat source.

Lightly grease a metal roasting or cooling rack and set on a baking sheet lined with aluminum foil. Put the lamb on the rack, fat-side down, and brush with half the reserved glaze. Broil until the top is browned and slightly charred in places, 10 to 12 minutes.

Flip the lamb and brush with the remaining 2 tablespoons glaze. Continue to broil until the top is browned and a meat thermometer inserted into the thickest part of the lamb registers 125°F, 10 to 12 minutes more. Since the meat is not the same thickness all over, some parts may char faster than others. If any section gets too dark, cover it with a piece of foil.

Transfer the lamb to a cutting board and let rest for 10 to 15 minutes. Cut into thin, bite-size slices and transfer to a platter. Spoon any glaze left on the baking sheet over the lamb.

Garnish the meat with scallions and sesame seeds. Serve with the lettuce, perilla leaves (if using), rice, lettuce wrap sauce, and pickles. To assemble, put a lettuce leaf in one hand and top with a perilla leaf (if using), a spoonful of rice, a smear of sauce, a piece of lamb, and some pickles. Wrap the lettuce around the ingredients and enjoy.

PORK

# PORK BELLY AND KIMCHI STIR-FRY WITH TOFU

## *DUBU KIMCHI*

**SERVES 4**

Kimchi and pork love each other. The pork really soaks up the flavor of the kimchi and the tofu adds a great soft texture. I made this dish often in college, as the ingredients are really cheap! I still order it quite often in restaurants because it is so good.

---

**12 ounces thinly sliced skinless pork belly, cut crosswise into 2-inch pieces**

**1 small onion, thinly sliced**

**6 cloves garlic, grated or minced**

**3 scallions, cut into 2-inch pieces**

**2 tablespoons *gochujang* (Korean chile paste)**

**2 tablespoons soy sauce**

**1 tablespoon sugar**

**1 tablespoon toasted sesame oil**

**Freshly ground black pepper**

**1 (14-ounce) package medium-firm tofu, drained and halved crosswise**

**2 tablespoons vegetable oil**

**2 cups packed drained Cabbage Kimchi (page 28), cut into 1-inch strips**

For Serving:

**Toasted sesame oil**

**Handful of finely chopped fresh chives, or handful of thinly sliced scallions**

**Roasted or black sesame seeds**

**Steamed White Rice (page 106)**

IN A MEDIUM BOWL, toss together the pork, onion, garlic, scallions, chile paste, soy sauce, sugar, sesame oil, and pepper to taste. Let marinate for about 15 minutes.

Put the tofu in a small saucepan, add enough water to just cover, and bring to a boil over high heat. Reduce the heat to maintain a simmer until heated through, 3 to 4 minutes. Drain, cut each piece of tofu in half to form triangles, then slice each triangle into thirds to form three triangles. You should have twelve triangles total. Return the tofu to the empty pot and cover to keep warm.

In a large skillet, heat the vegetable oil over medium-high heat. Add the pork mixture and cook, stirring continuously, until the pork is cooked through, 3 to 4 minutes. Add the kimchi and continue to cook, stirring often, 4 to 5 minutes more.

Transfer the pork and kimchi stir-fry to a platter and arrange the tofu triangles around it. Drizzle with a little sesame oil, top with the chives and sesame seeds, and serve with rice.

---

TIP: *This is a great way to use up well-fermented and funky cabbage kimchi, but a fresh young kimchi works fine as well.*

# ROASTED PORK BELLY LETTUCE WRAPS

*BOSSAM*

**SERVES 4 TO 6**

Sharing is a common theme underlying all of Korean food. *Bossam* embodies this convivial sentiment—everyone sharing from the same plate, yet creating a small bespoke parcel for their own consumption. The lettuce leaves and pickles cut the fat nicely and bring a welcome freshness to the dish. If your pork belly comes with the ribs on, cut them off and slather with some do*enjang*-honey-ginger-*gochujang* paste (make extra). Roast until cooked through and caramelized and you'll have the tastiest ribs ever.

**4 tablespoons *doenjang* (Korean soybean paste)**

**1 (3- to 3½-pound) boneless skin-on pork belly**

**1 onion, cut into eighths**

**8 cloves garlic, crushed**

**7 scallions, coarsely chopped**

**6 thick slices unpeeled fresh ginger**

**2 tablespoons honey**

**1½ tablespoons grated peeled fresh ginger**

**1 teaspoon *gochujang* (Korean chile paste)**

For Serving:

**Red or green lettuce leaves**

**Perilla leaves (*ggaennip*), also known as sesame leaves (optional)**

**Steamed White Rice (page 106)**

**Lettuce Wrap Sauce (page 213)**

**1 recipe Spicy Pickled Radish Salad (page 34)**

IN A LARGE, wide, heavy-bottomed saucepan, whisk together 2 tablespoons of the soybean paste and 1 cup water until smooth. Add the pork belly, skin-side up, the onion, garlic, scallions, sliced ginger, and enough water to cover the pork.

Bring to a boil over high heat and then reduce the heat to maintain a simmer until the pork is cooked through and very soft, about 2 hours. Transfer the pork belly to a baking sheet lined with aluminum foil and let cool. Discard the cooking liquid. When the pork is cool enough to handle, remove the skin (but not the fat) and discard.

Preheat the oven to 350°F.

Meanwhile, in a small bowl, whisk together the remaining 2 tablespoons soybean paste, honey, grated ginger, and chile paste until smooth and then smear the paste all over the top (skin side) of the pork belly. Roast the pork until the top is nicely caramelized, about 30 minutes. You can also broil the pork briefly for a little more char, if you like.

Let the pork rest in a warm place for about 15 minutes. Transfer to a cutting board and thinly slice into two-bite pieces. Serve the pork on a platter with the lettuce, perilla leaves (if using), rice, sauce, and pickled radish on the side. To assemble, put a lettuce leaf in one hand and top with a perilla leaf (if using), a spoonful of rice, a smear of sauce, a piece of pork, and some pickled radish. Wrap the lettuce around the ingredients and take a bite. You'll love it.

# KOREAN PULLED PORK

**MAKES ABOUT 6 CUPS**

I use this pulled pork recipe for my Korean Pulled Pork Quesadillas (page 204), Pulled Pork Chilaquiles (page 203), and Kimchi Pulled Pork Disco Fries (page 85). It can also be used in fried rice and bibimbap or topped with a fried egg and served with rice.

½ cup orange juice

2 tablespoons soy sauce

2 tablespoons *doenjang* (Korean soybean paste)

2 tablespoons *gochujang* (Korean chile paste)

1½ teaspoons *gochugaru* (Korean chile flakes)

3 limes, halved

4 pounds boneless pork butt, cut into 2- to 3-inch pieces and trimmed of excess fat

1 large onion, quartered

1 large navel orange, halved

5 cloves garlic, smashed

1 (2-inch) knob fresh ginger, thickly sliced and smashed

Kosher salt or sea salt

Freshly ground black pepper

PREHEAT THE OVEN to 300°F.

In a large, wide, oven-safe heavy-bottomed pot, whisk together the orange juice, soy sauce, soybean paste, chile paste, chile flakes, the juice of 1 lime, and 2 cups water until smooth. Add the pork, onion, orange halves, garlic, and ginger and stir to combine. Bring to a boil over high heat and then reduce the heat to maintain a simmer for about 10 minutes. Cover the pot and transfer to the oven. Cook, stirring halfway through, until the meat is very tender and falls apart easily, 2 to 2½ hours.

Using a slotted spoon or tongs, transfer the meat to a large shallow bowl. Pass the braising liquid through a fine-mesh strainer into another large, wide, heavy-bottomed pot (or strain it into a bowl and then return it to the same pot), discard the solids, and skim off the fat. Bring the liquid to a gentle boil and cook until it has reduced by half (about 1¼ cups), 10 to 15 minutes. Set aside.

Preheat the broiler and position a rack 4 to 5 inches from the heat source. Line a baking sheet with aluminum foil.

When the pork is cool enough to handle, coarsely shred the meat with your fingers or two forks, discarding any bits of fat. Transfer the pork to the prepared baking sheet. Drizzle with the reduced liquid, season with salt and pepper, and gently toss. Spread the pork in an even layer and broil until the meat is lightly charred and crisped in spots, about 6 minutes.

Squeeze the juice from the remaining 2 limes (or to taste) over the pork, toss, and serve.

# PULLED PORK CHILAQUILES

**SERVES 4 TO 6**

I first made chilaquiles while working in the test kitchen at *Saveur* magazine. My Korean twist below makes for a ridiculously sinful plate of deliciousness.

1½ pounds ripe tomatoes

4 jalapeños

1 tablespoon vegetable oil

1 large white onion, chopped

10 large sprigs fresh cilantro, including the stems

3 cloves garlic

1 tablespoon *gochujang* (Korean chile paste)

Kosher salt or sea salt

2 cups Korean Pulled Pork (page 202)

8 ounces tortilla chips

1 cup drained Cabbage Kimchi (page 28), chopped

¾ cup sour cream

½ cup crumbled Cotija or feta cheese

⅓ cup fresh cilantro leaves

Handful of thinly sliced scallions (optional)

PREHEAT THE BROILER and position a rack 4 to 5 inches from the heat source. Line a baking sheet with aluminum foil.

Put the tomatoes and jalapeños on the prepared baking sheet and broil on both sides until blistered and blackened in spots, about 10 minutes. Set aside to cool while you cook the onion. In a large, wide, heavy-bottomed pot, heat the oil over medium heat. Add the onion and cook, stirring occasionally, until soft, about 8 minutes. Remove from the heat.

Peel the skins from the tomatoes and jalapeños. Quarter the tomatoes and remove the stems from the jalapeños. For a milder effect, remove the ribs and seeds from the jalapeños, too. In a blender, combine about one-third of the tomatoes, all the jalapeños, half the onion, the cilantro, garlic, chile paste, and salt to taste and process until smooth. Add the remaining tomatoes and pulse until they are just liquefied.

Add the tomato mixture and pulled pork to the remaining onions in the pot, bring to a simmer, and cook until the pork is heated through, about 2 minutes. Add the tortilla chips and stir until coated and just softened, 1 to 2 minutes. Spread the chilaquiles on a large shallow platter and top with the kimchi, sour cream, Cotija, cilantro leaves, and scallions, if desired.

# KOREAN PULLED PORK QUESADILLAS

**SERVES 2**

Having lived in California for a number of years, I am a huge fan of Mexican food. Still, even when I just have a layover in CA, I will make the effort to find a taco stand or truck. Quesadillas are an all-time favorite. My Korean version will not disappoint.

2 (8-inch) flour tortillas

¼ cup grated Monterey Jack cheese

¼ cup grated aged Comté cheese

1½ cups Korean Pulled Pork (page 202)

¼ cup drained Cabbage Kimchi (page 28), chopped

1 tablespoon finely chopped fresh chives

2 teaspoons vegetable oil

For Serving:

Sour cream

Chopped fresh cilantro

Finely chopped tomatoes

Sliced pickled jalapeños, drained

Sliced avocado

LAY THE TORTILLAS on a clean, flat surface. On the bottom half of each tortilla, layer a quarter of the two cheeses, half the pork, half the kimchi, half the chives, and then another quarter of the two cheeses. (Putting cheese on both the top and bottom helps "glue" the quesadilla shut as it melts.) Fold the top half of the tortillas over the bottom half to enclose the fillings, pressing down firmly.

In a large nonstick skillet, heat the oil over medium heat. Carefully put the quesadillas in the skillet and cook, flipping halfway through, until the cheese is fully melted and the tortillas are golden brown, 3 to 4 minutes total. Let cool slightly.

Cut each quesadilla into wedges and top with some sour cream, cilantro, tomatoes, jalapeños, and avocado.

# PORK TACOS

**MAKES 16 SMALL TACOS**

I offered these Korean tacos at Jinjuu in London, and they have now become a menu staple. The meat is flavored with sesame oil, sesame seeds, and chile paste and is topped with both an Asian-style slaw and our homemade Cabbage Kimchi (page 28), which gives a deep savory flavor and a much welcomed crunch, freshness, and bite. Here, I use tenderloin, but thinly sliced pork belly works amazingly well too. Korean tacos are spreading across the globe, and it's not hard to see why.

Asian-Style Slaw:

¼ cup mayonnaise, preferably Kewpie or a Korean brand

3 tablespoons sour cream

2 tablespoons fresh lemon juice

2 teaspoons toasted sesame oil

1 teaspoon *gochugaru* (Korean chile flakes)

Kosher salt or sea salt

4 cups tightly packed thinly sliced green cabbage

1 cup julienned peeled tart apple or Asian pear

½ cup thinly sliced red onion

Pork:

3 tablespoons soy sauce

1 tablespoon toasted sesame oil

1 tablespoon mirin or lemon-lime soda

2 cloves garlic, grated or minced

1 tablespoon roasted sesame seeds

1 tablespoon *gochujang* (Korean chile paste)

Kosher salt or sea salt

1 teaspoon freshly ground black pepper

1 pound pork tenderloin, partially frozen, then thinly sliced crosswise

1 tablespoon vegetable oil

For Serving:

16 small (6-inch) corn tortillas

Finely chopped Cabbage Kimchi (page 28), drained

Thinly sliced avocado

Quartered cherry or grape tomatoes

Sour cream

Finely chopped fresh chives

**FOR THE SLAW:** In a large bowl, stir together the mayonnaise, sour cream, lemon juice, sesame oil, chile flakes, and salt to taste. Add the cabbage, apple, and onion and toss to coat. Cover and refrigerate.

**FOR THE PORK:** In a large bowl, stir together the soy sauce, sesame oil, mirin, garlic, sesame seeds, chili paste, a pinch of salt, and the pepper. Add the pork and toss to coat. Let marinate for about 1 hour at room temperature or cover and refrigerate up to overnight.

Before cooking, heat the tortillas on a hot dry skillet or griddle, flipping halfway through, until puffed and blistered in spots, 4 to 6 minutes. Keep warm wrapped in a clean kitchen towel.

In a large skillet, heat the vegetable oil over medium-high heat. Add the pork mixture and cook, stirring often, until the pork loses its pink-ness, about 3 minutes. Transfer the pork to a platter and serve with the tortillas, Asian-style slaw, kimchi, avocado, tomatoes, sour cream, and chives.

# SPICY PORK BELLY CHEESESTEAK

**SERVES 2**

Cheesesteaks are a go-to food item for me, like a burger or a taco. You have to love that thin meat, onions, and cheese chucked into a soft roll. Do try to get the right bread, as it makes a big difference. I know the classic cheesesteak uses Cheez Whiz. . . . But I can't . . . I just can't. I've also swapped in pork instead of beef here, just to keep it interesting. These cheesesteaks were the biggest hit when we were filming. They didn't last one minute after the camera stopped rolling.

**2 cloves garlic, grated or minced**

**1 tablespoon *gochujang* (Korean chile paste)**

**1 tablespoon mirin**

**1 tablespoon soy sauce**

**1 teaspoon grated peeled fresh ginger**

**1 teaspoon toasted sesame oil**

**10 ounces thinly sliced skinless pork belly**

**2 (6-inch) soft Italian rolls, split**

**2 tablespoons unsalted butter, at room temperature**

**1 tablespoon vegetable oil**

**1 small onion, thinly sliced**

**4 button mushrooms, thinly sliced**

**2 fresh Korean green chiles or jalapeños, seeded and thinly sliced on an angle**

**4 ounces sliced provolone cheese**

For Serving:

**1 scallion, thinly sliced on an angle**

**Roasted sesame seeds**

***Gochugaru* (Korean chile flakes)**

**Sliced pickled jalapeños, drained**

IN A MEDIUM BOWL, stir together the garlic, chile paste, mirin, soy sauce, ginger, and sesame oil. Add the pork and let marinate at room temperature for about 30 minutes or cover and refrigerate up to overnight.

Preheat the oven to 200°F.

Heat a large skillet over medium-high heat. Spread the cut sides of the rolls with the butter. Working in batches, if needed, toast the rolls cut-side down, gently pressing on them so the centers toast as well, until lightly golden, about 1 minute. Transfer the rolls to the oven to keep warm.

Wipe out the skillet and return it to the stove. Add the vegetable oil and heat over medium-high heat. Add the pork and cook, stirring occasionally, until the meat is cooked through and golden and lightly charred in spots, about 5 minutes. Add the onion, mushrooms, and chiles and cook, stirring occasionally, until the onions and mushrooms have softened slightly, about 2 minutes. Divide the mixture into two mounds in the skillet and top each mound with half the cheese. Cover the skillet and cook just until the cheese melts, about 1 minute.

Scoop each mound onto a roll, sprinkle with some scallions, sesame seeds, chile flakes, and pickled jalapeños. Serve immediately.

SAUCES

# PANCAKE DIPPING SAUCE

## *CHOGANJANG*

### MAKES ABOUT ½ CUP

This versatile, ubiquitous sauce can be used for all the pancakes in the book, including the Panfried Zucchini, Mushroom, and Tofu (page 49), Panfried Fish (page 52), Seafood Fritters (page 53), and Lotus Root and Beef Patties (page 75).

¼ cup soy sauce

1½ tablespoons rice vinegar

1 tablespoon toasted sesame oil

1 tablespoon crushed roasted sesame seeds

1 tablespoon *gochugaru* (Korean chile flakes)

2 scallions, very thinly sliced on an angle

IN A SMALL BOWL, stir together all the ingredients. Cover and store in the refrigerator if not using immediately.

# CHILE-SOY DIPPING SAUCE

## *YANGNYUM GANJANG*

### MAKES ABOUT ½ CUP

This sauce is my go-to sauce for dumplings, such as my Meaty Dumplings (page 54) and King Dumplings (page 56).

6 tablespoons soy sauce

2½ tablespoons Korean apple vinegar (*sagwa-shikcho*) or rice vinegar

1 tablespoon thinly sliced fresh Korean red chile or Fresno chile (sliced on an angle)

4½ teaspoons toasted sesame oil

2 teaspoons roasted sesame seeds

2 scallions, very thinly sliced on an angle

IN A SMALL BOWL, stir together all the ingredients. Cover and store in the refrigerator if not using immediately.

# LETTUCE WRAP SAUCE

*SSAMJANG*

**MAKES ABOUT ⅔ CUP**

This strong, pungent sauce is used in my Roasted Pork Belly Lettuce Wrap (page 200) and Doenjang-Glazed Lamb Lettuce Wraps (page 194). It can also be used as a dip for crudités and is especially good with raw garlic slices and small napa cabbage leaves. There are many variations on *ssamjang* sauces—another version is my Spicy Lettuce Wrap Sauce (right).

**6 tablespoons *doenjang* (Korean soybean paste)**

**2 tablespoons toasted sesame oil**

**2 tablespoons grated onion**

**2 tablespoons roasted sesame seeds**

**1 tablespoon grated peeled fresh ginger**

IN A SMALL BOWL, whisk together all the ingredients until smooth. Cover and store in the refrigerator if not using immediately.

# SPICY LETTUCE WRAP SAUCE

*GOCHUJANG SSAMJANG*

**MAKES ABOUT 1½ CUPS**

Use this sauce for BBQ Beef Short Ribs (page 189) or any barbecued meat in general. I also like to spice up Doenjang Mayonnaise (page 216) with a spoonful or two. It also does wonders when stirred into regular mayo. I serve this combo with Chicken Skewers (page 169) and everything from French fries to crudités. This is the best hot sauce ever, and I find myself wanting to smear it on everything.

**½ cup plus 1 tablespoon *doenjang* (Korean soybean paste)**

**¼ cup *gochujang* (Korean chile paste)**

**¼ cup mirin**

**2 tablespoons roasted sesame seeds**

**1 tablespoon toasted sesame oil**

**2 cloves garlic, grated or minced**

**2 scallions, thinly sliced on an angle**

IN A SMALL BOWL, whisk together all the ingredients until smooth. Cover and store in the refrigerator if not using immediately.

# GOCHUJANG SAUCE

## *CHOGOCHUJANG*

**MAKES A SCANT ½ CUP**

This ubiquitous Korean hot sauce is used for the Mixed Rice Bowl with Beef (page 107) and can be used anywhere you want to add a touch of heat.

3 tablespoons *gochujang* (Korean chile paste)

2½ tablespoons mirin

2 teaspoons sugar

2 teaspoons roasted sesame seeds

1 teaspoon toasted sesame oil

1 teaspoon thinly sliced scallions (sliced on an angle)

IN A SMALL BOWL, stir together all the ingredients. Cover and store in the refrigerator if not using immediately.

# GOCHUJANG GLAZE

**MAKES ABOUT ½ CUP**

This glaze is similar to Gochujang Sauce (left), but is generally broiled on various proteins—Gochujang-Glazed Salmon (page 157), tofu, meatballs, ribs—rather than used as a dip or spread.

3 tablespoons *gochujang* (Korean chile paste)

2 tablespoons mirin

2 tablespoons soy sauce

2 tablespoons sugar

½ tablespoon toasted sesame oil

2 cloves garlic, grated or minced

1 teaspoon grated peeled fresh ginger

1 teaspoon freshly ground black pepper

IN A SMALL BOWL, stir together all the ingredients. Cover and store in the refrigerator if not using immediately.

Chile-Soy Dipping Sauce

Spicy Korean Mustard
Vinaigrette

Kimchi and Chive
Hollandaise Sauce

Gochujang Glaze

Doenjang Mayonnaise

# DOENJANG GLAZE

**MAKES ABOUT 1¼ CUPS**

This savory, salty, and slightly sweet mixture is used in the Doenjang-Glazed Lamb Lettuce Wraps (page 194) and Doenjang-Glazed Broiled Asian Eggplant (page 103).

½ cup *doenjang* (Korean soybean paste)

¼ cup honey

5 cloves garlic, grated or minced

3 scallions, thinly sliced on an angle

2 tablespoons soy sauce

2 tablespoons toasted sesame oil

IN A SMALL BOWL, whisk together all the ingredients until smooth. Cover and store in the refrigerator if not using immediately.

# DOENJANG MAYONNAISE

**MAKES ABOUT ½ CUP**

Use this simple, umami-rich condiment as a dipping sauce for Mom's BBQ Chicken (page 174), slathered on the Krazy Korean Burgers (page 185) or grilled corn, and pretty much anywhere else you would use mayo.

½ cup mayonnaise, preferably Kewpie or a Korean brand

1 tablespoon *doenjang* (Korean soybean paste)

IN A SMALL BOWL, whisk together the mayonnaise and soybean paste until smooth. Cover and store in the refrigerator if not using immediately.

# KOREAN KETCHUP

**MAKES ABOUT ½ CUP**

Use this on burgers, like my Krazy Korean Burgers (page 185), and as a dipping sauce for fries and Chile Bombs (page 78).

6 tablespoons ketchup

4 teaspoons *gochujang* (Korean chile paste)

IN A SMALL BOWL, stir together the ketchup and chile paste. Cover and store in the refrigerator if not using immediately.

# SPICY KOREAN MUSTARD VINAIGRETTE

**MAKES ABOUT 5 TABLESPOONS**

I adore the spicy mustard dressing used to season the salad from the Ice-Cold Noodles (page 119) so much that I decided to turn it into a full-on vinaigrette. Use it for the Frisée, Persimmon, Pomegranate, and Feta Salad (page 97), the Spicy Tuna Tartare (page 73), or anywhere else you like.

2½ tablespoons rice vinegar

1 tablespoon extra-virgin olive oil

½ tablespoon toasted sesame oil

2 teaspoons prepared Korean mustard (*gyeoja*) or English mustard

1 teaspoon superfine sugar

Kosher salt or sea salt

Freshly ground black pepper

IN A SMALL BOWL, whisk together all the ingredients until the sugar has dissolved and the vinaigrette is emulsified. Cover and store in the refrigerator if not using immediately.

# KIMCHI AND CHIVE HOLLANDAISE SAUCE

**MAKES ABOUT ¾ CUP**

Kimchi liquid gives this hollandaise a slight kick. Serve it as you would any hollandaise, with crab cakes, steak, eggs Benedict, poached salmon, or steamed vegetables, such as asparagus or green beans.

10 tablespoons (1 stick plus 2 tablespoons) unsalted butter, cut into cubes

2 large egg yolks

5 teaspoons kimchi liquid from Cabbage Kimchi (page 28)

1 tablespoon fresh lemon juice

¼ teaspoon kosher salt or sea salt

*Gochugaru* (Korean chile flakes)

1 tablespoon finely chopped fresh chives

IN A SMALL saucepan, melt the butter over medium heat. Transfer to a glass measuring cup for easy pouring, if you like.

In a blender, combine the egg yolks, kimchi liquid, lemon juice, salt, and chile flakes to taste (start with a small pinch) and blend until mixed. With the motor running on low speed, slowly pour in all but about 2 tablespoons of the melted butter and blend until a creamy sauce forms. It should be fairly loose. If you prefer a thicker hollandaise, with the motor running, slowly pour in the remaining butter and blend until incorporated. Stir in the chives and serve immediately.

TIP: *To hold the hollandaise sauce for up to 2 hours or so, store it in a warmed thermos.*

# BREAD

Koreans don't have a tradition of bread baking, but in recent times, Korean style French bakeries have been popping up all over Korea and the world. I find making bread extremely therapeutic and could not resist having a chapter dedicated to this craft in my book.

# GOUGÈRES WITH KOREAN MUSTARD
## *AND BLACK SESAME SEEDS*

**MAKES ABOUT 36 GOUGÈRES**

I remember making my first batch of gougères at my cooking school, the French Culinary Institute (now the International Culinary Center) in Soho, NYC. Since then, pâte à choux has become one of my favorite doughs to make and eat. Here, I have given these cheese puffs a little Seoul by adding Korean mustard and *gochugaru*. Feel free to use this recipe as a base as well, and create your own flavors.

½ cup plus 2 tablespoons (148 milliliters) milk

3 teaspoons Korean mustard powder (*gyeoja*) or English mustard

8 tablespoons (1 stick / 113 grams) unsalted butter, cut into cubes

1 teaspoon kosher salt or sea salt

½ teaspoon *gochugaru* (Korean chile flakes)

1 cup (120 grams) all-purpose flour

4 large eggs, at room temperature

1½ cups grated Gruyère cheese (about 85 grams)

2 tablespoons black sesame seeds

PREHEAT THE OVEN to 400°F. Line two baking sheets with parchment paper.

Stir together 2 tablespoons of the milk with 1 teaspoon of the mustard until smooth. Set aside.

In a medium saucepan, combine the remaining ½ cup milk, 2 teaspoons mustard, the butter, salt, chile flakes, and ½ cup water. Heat over medium-high heat until the butter melts. Remove the pan from the heat, add the flour, and stir vigorously with a wooden spoon until the mixture pulls away from the sides of the pan, 1 to 2 minutes. Return the pan to the heat for a minute, stirring continuously.

Transfer the dough to the bowl of a stand mixer fitted with the paddle attachment. Beat the dough on medium speed for a minute or two to cool it slightly. Beat in the eggs one at a time, making sure each egg is fully incorporated and the dough is smooth before adding the next. After the last egg is added, continue beating the dough until it is thick, shiny, and smooth. Add 1 cup of the cheese and beat until combined.

Drop tablespoons of the dough onto the prepared baking sheets, leaving about 1 inch of space between them. Brush the tops with the reserved milk mixture and then sprinkle with the sesame seeds and remaining ½ cup cheese. Bake for 20 to 22 minutes, until the gougères have doubled in size and become golden. Serve warm or at room temperature.

Spicy Sesame Straws and Gougères
with Korean Mustard (page 221)

# SPICY SESAME STRAWS

**MAKES 16 TO 18 STRAWS**

My head pastry chef, Jaime Garbutt, and I made these twists for Seoul Gourmet. The Korean-flavor-infused breads were such a hit that many patrons were asking to pack them up to go. These sesame straws are flavored with *ssamjang*, a spicy sauce served with lettuce wraps (*bossam*) and many other foods. (Note that the *ssamjang* below isn't the same as the one on page 213; there are lots of variations and I think this is best for the straws.) It gives conventional puff pastry straws a bright punch. If possible, use an all-butter puff pastry.

2 tablespoons *gochujang* (Korean chile paste)

1 tablespoon *doenjang* (Korean soybean paste)

1 tablespoon mirin

1 tablespoon honey

2 teaspoons crushed roasted sesame seeds

1 teaspoon garlic powder

1 teaspoon toasted sesame oil

All-purpose flour, for dusting

1 (14-ounce / 390-gram) sheet puff pastry, halved crosswise

1 large egg, lightly beaten with a splash of water

3 tablespoons roasted sesame seeds

3 tablespoons black sesame seeds

IN A VERY SMALL BOWL, whisk together the chile paste, soybean paste, mirin, honey, crushed roasted sesame seeds, garlic powder, and sesame oil until smooth. Set the mixture aside.

Lightly flour a clean work surface. Roll one piece of the puff pastry into a 10 x 14-inch rectangle and set aside. Roll the other piece into a 10 x 14-inch rectangle and spread the chile paste mixture on top, keeping a ½-inch border. Set the other rectangle on top, matching up the edges, and very gently roll to seal the pieces together.

Brush with the egg mixture, avoiding the edges so the layers of pastry don't stick together during baking, and sprinkle with half the roasted and black sesame seeds. Lightly press the seeds in with your hands. Carefully flip the pastry over onto one of the prepared baking sheets, brush with the egg mixture, and sprinkle with the remaining roasted and black sesame seeds, lightly pressing them in with your hands. Refrigerate for about 15 minutes, until firm enough to handle.

Preheat the oven to 350°F. Position the oven racks in the upper and lower thirds of the oven. Line three baking sheets with parchment paper.

Using a pizza wheel or floured knife, trim the edges as needed to neaten them. Cut the pastry lengthwise into ½-inch-thick strips. Gently twist each strip until it resembles a loose corkscrew and transfer to the prepared baking sheets, spacing them about 1½ inches apart. Chill for 20 minutes. Bake for 20 to 22 minutes, rotating the pans halfway through, until golden. Let the sesame straws cool on the baking sheets and serve at room temperature.

# KIMCHI AND BACON BRIOCHE

**MAKES 2 LOAVES**

Kimchi may seem like a strange ingredient to add to boulangerie, but kimchi bread is actually a popular item in Korean bakeries. Bacon is a natural pairing for both kimchi and bread, so why not combine them all? At the first restaurant I ran in London, Jaime Garbutt, my head pastry chef, made this brioche in roll form for our bread basket, and people raved about them. For the most kimchi flavor, use a nicely fermented funky kimchi. Swapping half the milk with kimchi liquid also helps increase the kimchi flavor, but it's also fine to just use regular kimchi.

8 ounces (227 grams) unsmoked bacon, chopped

½ cup (118 milliliters) milk

4½ cups (542 grams) all-purpose flour, plus more as needed

2 tablespoons sugar

1 tablespoon kosher salt or sea salt

2 teaspoons instant yeast

5 large eggs, lightly beaten

8 tablespoons (1 stick / 113 grams) unsalted butter, cut into cubes, at room temperature

1 cup (227 grams) drained and finely chopped Cabbage Kimchi (page 28), patted dry

1 large egg, lightly beaten with a splash of water (egg wash)

IN A LARGE SKILLET, cook the bacon over medium heat, stirring occasionally, until crisp, about 10 minutes. Transfer to a paper towel–lined plate to drain and cool.

Meanwhile, in a very small saucepan, heat the milk to about 105°F. In the bowl of a stand mixer fitted with the dough hook, combine the flour, sugar, salt, and yeast and mix on low speed. Add the eggs and warmed milk and beat on medium speed until a smooth but sticky ball of dough forms, about 5 minutes. With the mixer running on low speed, gradually add the butter piece by piece, waiting for each piece to be incorporated before adding the next, then mix until the dough completely pulls away from the sides of the bowl and becomes very smooth and supple, 8 to 10 minutes more.

Add the kimchi and bacon to the dough and beat on low speed until well incorporated. The dough should be slightly wet and tacky. Depending on how wet your kimchi was, you may need to add more flour. Mix in 1 tablespoon at a time, and add up to ¼ cup (30 grams) total, as needed. Shape the dough into a ball, transfer to a lightly greased bowl, and cover with a tea towel or plastic wrap. Set in a warm spot and let rise until doubled in size, about 2 hours.

Lightly grease two 8 x 4-inch loaf pans. Divide the dough in half and cover one piece with a tea towel or plastic wrap. On a lightly floured work surface, using lightly floured hands, pat the other piece into a rectangle and fold into thirds, as if folding

a letter. Pinch together the long seam to seal, then pinch the ends closed.

Fold the dough in half lengthwise. Again, pinch together the long seam to seal, then pinch the ends closed. Gently tuck the ends underneath the loaf. Put the loaf in the prepared pan seam-side down. Repeat the process with the remaining piece of dough and second pan. Lightly cover the pans with tea towels or plastic wrap, set in a warm spot, and let rise until the loaves are doubled in size, about 1½ hours.

Preheat the oven to 400°F.

Brush the tops of the loaves with the beaten egg wash mixture. Using a sharp serrated knife, make a long, shallow slash down the center of loaf. Bake for 40 minutes, until the tops are golden and the loaves sound hollow when tapped on the bottom (the internal temperature should be about 185°F). Remove the loaves from the pans, transfer to a wire rack, and let cool before slicing and serving.

# ROASTED BARLEY TEA SESAME BRAIDS

**MAKES 2 LOAVES**

These beautiful and delicious braided loaves contain both barley tea and the barley itself, which lends some chewy bits to the bread. For maximum flavor, I also brew the tea at a much higher concentration than I do for regular Roasted Barley Tea (page 264).

---

1 cup (103 grams) unhulled roasted barley

5 cups (625 grams) bread flour, plus more for dusting

¼ cup (72 grams) sugar

3 tablespoons powdered milk

2½ teaspoons instant yeast

2 teaspoons kosher salt or sea salt

1 large egg, lightly beaten (egg wash)

4 tablespoons (½ stick / 57 grams) unsalted butter, at room temperature

1 large egg, lightly beaten with a splash of water

1 tablespoon roasted sesame seeds

1 tablespoon black sesame seeds

IN A SMALL SAUCEPAN, combine the roasted barley and 3 cups water and bring to a boil over high heat. Reduce the heat to maintain a simmer until the liquid is a golden color, about 20 minutes. Pass the tea through a fine-mesh strainer into a bowl and reserve 1 cup of the spent barley. Measure 1⅓ cups (314 ml) of the tea and set aside to cool to about 105°F. Drink or discard any remaining tea.

In the bowl of a stand mixer fitted with the paddle attachment, combine the flour, sugar, powdered milk, yeast, and salt and mix on low speed. Add the lightly beaten egg, butter, and cooled tea and beat on low speed until a shaggy dough forms, about 1 minute. Replace the paddle with the dough hook and beat on medium speed until the dough is smooth and supple, about 5 minutes more. Add the reserved spent barley and mix until well incorporated. Shape the dough into a ball, transfer to a large greased bowl, and cover with a tea towel or plastic wrap. Set in a warm spot and let rise until doubled in size, about 1 hour.

Line two baking sheets with parchment paper. Divide the dough into six equal pieces and cover with a tea towel or plastic wrap. On a lightly floured work surface, using lightly floured hands, stretch and roll one piece of dough into a 12-inch-long rope with tapered ends. Lay the rope lengthwise in the center of one of the prepared baking sheets. Shape two more pieces of dough the same way.

Lay the ropes along each side of the first rope, with the tops together and the bottom ends fanning out slightly like a tent. Gather the three tops, firmly pinch them together, and tuck the end underneath the loaf. Position the baking sheet so that the tucked end is farthest away from you. To form the braid, lift the rope on the right and set it between the center and left rope, making it the new center rope. Take the rope on the left and set it between the center and right rope, making it the new center rope.

Continue braiding the ropes in this order until they are too short to braid anymore. Firmly pinch the bottoms of the ropes together like you did with the tops and then tuck the end underneath the loaf. Lightly cover the loaf with a tea towel or plastic wrap. Repeat the process with the remaining three pieces of dough on the other baking sheet and lightly cover. Set the baking sheets in a warm spot and let rise until the loaves are doubled in size, 45 to 60 minutes.

Preheat the oven to 400°F.

Brush the tops of the loaves with the beaten egg wash mixture and sprinkle with the roasted and black sesame seeds. Bake for 15 minutes, then reduce the oven temperature to 350°F. Bake for about 25 minutes more, tenting the loaves with aluminum foil if browning too quickly, until they are golden and sound hollow when tapped on the bottom. Transfer the loaves to a wire rack and let cool.

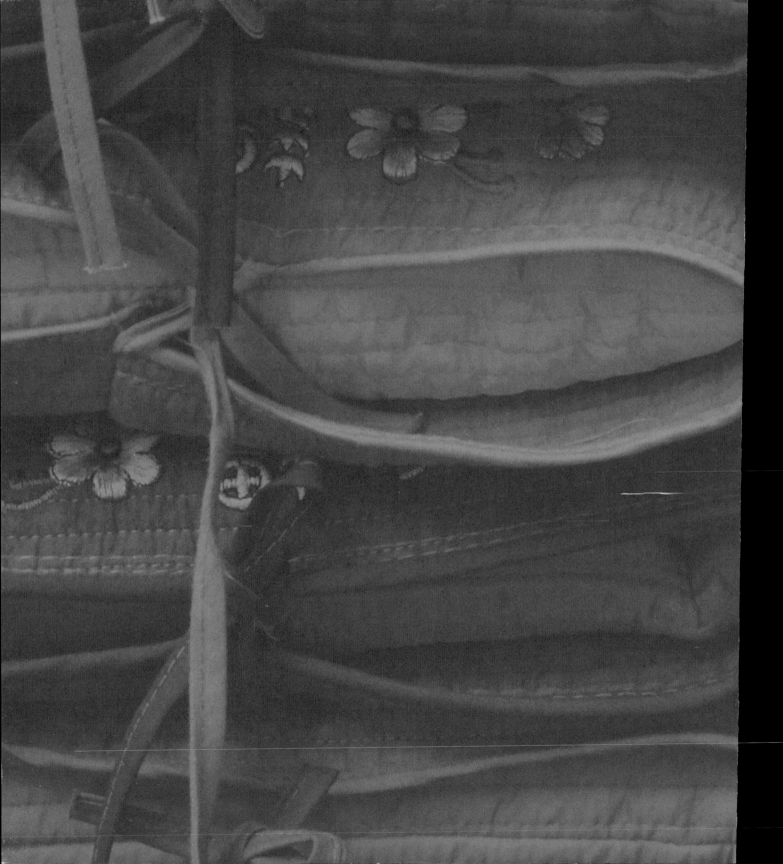

SWEETS

# DRUNKEN RICE FRO-YO

## MAKES ABOUT 1 QUART

*Makgeolli*—Korea's oldest alcoholic beverage, dating to the tenth century—is a milky, slightly sweet, and tangy unfiltered rice liquor that was originally made and drunk by farmers. With its low alcohol level, health benefits (it contains fiber, vitamins, and some of the good bacteria also found in yogurt), low price, and compatibility with high-flavored Korean food, however, it has seen a big increase in popularity in the country.

Although I like to drink it with a meal, *makgeolli* also adds a nice light, boozy touch to frozen yogurt. (Despite its low alcohol level, I'd still keep this dessert away from the kiddies.) Whether you're consuming it straight or using it in this recipe, gently shake the bottle before pouring it out so any sediment that has fallen to the bottom is reincorporated into the liquid. Refrigerate the bottle after opening and drink relatively quickly after opening to enjoy its freshness.

3 cups (680 grams) full-fat Greek yogurt

½ cup plus 2 tablespoons (140 grams) superfine sugar

1¼ cups (300 milliliters) shaken *makgeolli* (Korean rice liquor)

3 tablespoons honey

1 tablespoon fresh lemon juice

¼ teaspoon kosher salt or sea salt

Diced pineapple, for serving (optional)

Toasted coconut chips or shredded coconut, for serving (optional)

IN A LARGE BOWL, whisk together the yogurt, sugar, rice liquor, honey, lemon juice, and salt until the sugar has dissolved. Cover and refrigerate until well chilled, at least 1 hour.

Process in an ice cream maker according to the manufacturer's instructions. Serve immediately in bowls and top with pineapple and coconut, if desired. You can also transfer the yogurt to a quart container with a tight-fitting lid, press a piece of plastic wrap directly on the surface of the yogurt, and freeze to the desired firmness. Eat within 2 to 3 days, as the alcohol flavor intensifies as it sits.

TIP: *The richness of the frozen yogurt is dependent on the quality of the Greek yogurt, so use the thickest full-fat type you can find.*

# CINNAMON AND PERSIMMON PUNCH SORBET

## *SUJEONGGWA SORBET*

**MAKES ABOUT 1 QUART**

Cinnamon and Persimmon Punch (page 267) is so flavorful and sweet and tastes so great icy cold that it seems natural to transform it into sorbet. Like most dried fruits, dried persimmons are found in varying degrees of dryness. A moister one is preferred here, but if your persimmon is very dry, you can use one that was soaked in the punch. (Note that in Korean markets, dried persimmons are often kept in the produce section.)

**3¾ cups (887 milliliters) strained
Cinnamon and Persimmon Punch
(page 267), chilled well**

**1 dried persimmon (see note above),
stem removed and cut into small pieces
(about ⅓ cup)**

**2 tablespoons fresh lemon juice**

**Pinch of kosher salt or sea salt**

**Crystallized Lemon Zest (page 261),
for serving (optional)**

**Finely chopped candied ginger,
for serving (optional)**

IN A MEDIUM BOWL, stir together the punch, dried persimmon, lemon juice, and salt. Process in an ice cream maker according to the manufacturer's instructions. Transfer the sorbet to a quart container with a tight-fitting lid, press a piece of plastic wrap directly on the surface of the sorbet, and freeze to the desired firmness.

To serve, scoop the sorbet into bowls and garnish with crystallized lemon zest and candied ginger, if desired.

# CARAMEL DOENJANG ICE CREAM

## MAKES ABOUT 1 QUART

Salted caramel is one of my favorite flavor combinations. I love how the salt cuts through the sweetness. In this rich, creamy ice cream, the *doenjang* is the salty element. Eat the ice cream as is or, for true decadence, scoop it on top of an equally rich square of Korean Coffee Brownies (page 253). As *doenjang* can vary in strength, adjust as necessary to your taste, or substitute red miso, which is lighter in flavor.

1 cup (229 grams) sugar

2¼ cups (540 milliliters) heavy cream

¼ cup (62 grams) *doenjang* (Korean soybean paste)

1 cup (240 milliliters) whole milk

3 large eggs

IN A MEDIUM saucepan that can hold at least 6 cups, combine the sugar and ½ cup water and bring to a boil over medium-high heat without stirring. Swirl the pan occasionally after it comes to a boil, until the sugar melts and turns a dark amber color, 10 to 12 minutes. Slowly and carefully whisk in 1¼ cups of the cream. (The mixture will bubble up in the pan, which is why you need a larger saucepan than you may think.) The caramel will seize up, then melt again. Whisk until the caramel dissolves completely. Whisk in the soybean paste and set the caramel aside.

In a small saucepan, whisk together the milk and remaining 1 cup cream over medium heat until the mixture starts to steam. Remove it from the heat before it comes to a boil and set aside. In a medium bowl, whisk the eggs until combined, then slowly whisk in half of the hot milk mixture in a steady stream. Pour the egg-milk mixture back into the saucepan.

Return the saucepan to the stove and heat over medium heat, stirring continuously, until the custard coats the back of a wooden spoon. Be sure to stir continuously and don't let the custard boil. Pass the custard through a fine-mesh strainer into the saucepan with the caramel and stir to combine. Strain the mixture again into a container with a tight-fitting lid and let cool. Cover and refrigerate until very cold.

Process in an ice cream maker according to the manufacturer's instructions. Transfer the ice cream to a quart container with a tight-fitting lid, press a piece of plastic wrap directly on the surface of the ice cream, and freeze to the desired firmness.

TIP: *If the egg-milk mixture gets too hot while you're whisking it and curdles, immediately pour it into a blender and process until smooth. As long as the custard doesn't taste too eggy, you can proceed to the next step.*

# BOOZY PLUM GRANITA

**SERVES 8**

I ate my first real granita overlooking the jagged cliffs of Positano on Italy's Amalfi Coast. It was a tart lemon granita made from the famed local lemons. The coarse crystals made for a light yet satisfying dessert. Korea hardly has a history of making granita, but its rich sweet plum wine, *maesil ju*, combined with sweet juicy plums does this dessert proud.

1¾ pounds (794 grams) ripe red plums, pitted and cut into chunks

¾ cup (160 grams) sugar, plus more if needed

Kosher salt or sea salt

1 cup (240 milliliters) plum wine (*maesil ju*)

2 tablespoons fresh lemon juice

Crystallized Lemon Zest (page 261), for serving (optional)

PUT THE PLUMS in a medium heavy-bottomed pot. Add the sugar, using more as needed depending on how sweet your fruit is, and a pinch of salt and toss together. Stir the mixture over medium heat until the sugar has dissolved and the plums start to release their juices. Raise the heat as needed to bring to a gentle simmer and cook, stirring often, until a chunky, bright-red puree forms, about 20 minutes.

Pass the mixture through a fine-mesh strainer into a large bowl, pressing down on the solids with the bottom of a ladle. Discard the solids. Add the wine, lemon juice, and 2½ cups (600 milliliters) water to the bowl with the puree and mix well. Pour the mixture into a freezer-safe glass or nonreactive 9 x 13-inch baking dish and transfer to the freezer, uncovered.

After 3 hours, the granita should be slushy in the center and icy at the edges of the dish. Use a fork to break up and mix the icier portions, pulling them to the center of the dish. Return to the freezer for 1 to 2 hours more. Rake a fork over the surface and scrape to create flaky crystals. Return to the freezer and repeat as needed until the granita is light and fluffy. Cover with a lid or plastic wrap until ready to serve. Scoop the granita into bowls and top with the crystallized lemon zest.

# RED BEAN ICE POPS

**MAKES TEN 3-OUNCE ICE POPS**

These popsicles called "bi bi big" were a staple of my childhood—so yummy! When I eat them now, I trick myself into thinking that they're somewhat healthy since they are made with beans. I guess their protein content is higher than that of many ice pops, but that's about it!

Red bean ice cream is served in many Asian restaurants, but rarely are they served there in the form of an ice pop, which brings out people's inner child. My version doesn't involve true ice cream, but it is creamy and sweet with chunks of whole bean.

1¼ cups (340 grams) canned sweetened whole adzuki beans

1 cup (240 milliliters) whole milk

3 tablespoons sugar

Pinch of kosher salt or sea salt

1 cup (240 milliliters) heavy cream

IN A BLENDER, combine ¾ cup of the beans, the milk, sugar, and salt and process until completely smooth. Transfer the mixture to a medium bowl or a 4-cup spouted measuring cup for easy pouring and stir in the cream.

Divide the remaining ½ cup beans evenly among ten 3-ounce ice pop molds. Top with enough of the bean-cream mixture to fill each mold, allowing about ¼-inch headspace for expansion during freezing. Use a popsicle stick, chopstick, or knife to combine the beans with the liquid. Don't worry if the beans sink back to the bottom.

Assemble the covers and sticks for each mold. If your molds don't come with covers, you may need to let the mixture freeze for 30 minutes to an hour before you can insert the sticks without them popping up all askew. Freeze the ice pops until solid, 4 to 5 hours, before unmolding.

# SPICY MOLTEN CHOCOLATE LAVA CAKES

**SERVES 6**

Molten chocolate lava cakes have been around for decades, but they don't seem to lose their popularity. Thick chocolate oozing from a warm chocolate cake. What's not to like?

I spice up my lava cakes with *gochugaru*, Korean chile flakes. You can add more or less, depending on how much heat you want. I suggest starting with ¼ teaspoon and going from there.

---

**8 tablespoons (1 stick/113 grams) unsalted butter, cut into cubes, plus more for greasing the ramekins**

**2 teaspoons unsweetened cocoa powder**

**6 ounces (169 grams) bittersweet chocolate, chopped**

**2 teaspoons instant espresso powder**

**¼ teaspoon *gochugaru* (Korean chile flakes), or to taste, finely crushed**

**3 large eggs, at room temperature**

**2 large yolks, at room temperature**

**¾ cup (100 grams) confectioners' sugar**

**¾ teaspoon vanilla extract**

**½ teaspoon kosher salt or sea salt**

**¼ cup (28 grams) all-purpose flour**

**Whipped cream or vanilla ice cream, for serving**

PREHEAT THE OVEN to 450°F. Grease six ¾-cup ramekins or custard cups with butter. Put the cocoa into a ramekin and swirl it to coat the interior. Knock any excess into the next ramekin and continue the process until all the ramekins are coated. Put the ramekins on a baking sheet and set aside.

In the top of a double boiler, heat the butter, chocolate, espresso powder, and chile flakes over medium heat, stirring occasionally, until the chocolate and butter have melted and the mixture is smooth. Set the chocolate mixture aside to let cool slightly. Meanwhile, in a large bowl, beat the eggs, yolks, sugar, vanilla, and salt with a hand mixer on high speed until thick and pale, about 3 minutes.

Stir the chocolate mixture into the egg mixture and then fold in the flour. Divide the batter among the prepared ramekins and bake for 11 to 12 minutes, until the sides are set, but the center is soft to the touch. Keep an eye on them, as they can go from molten lava to barely runny in a matter of minutes. Let the cakes rest for 2 to 3 minutes and then run a thin knife between the cakes and the ramekins to loosen. Working with one ramekin at a time, set a plate over a ramekin, carefully invert, and remove the ramekin. Serve immediately, with whipped cream or ice cream.

---

**TIP:** *These cakes can be assembled ahead of time, covered, and refrigerated for several hours. Bring to room temperature before baking.*

# GREEN TEA CHIFFON CAKE

## MAKES ONE 10-INCH ANGEL FOOD–STYLE CAKE

This delicate cake is an adaptation of a chiffon cake made by the mom of my "Harvest Time in Harlem" cofounder, Yuri Asano. It's one of my "go-to" desserts to prepare when I'm entertaining because it's so easy, and it's the perfect end to a big meal. Don't skimp on the quality of the green tea powder, as the better ones not only taste more refined, but lend a gorgeous color and fragrance. Less expensive varieties tend to make the cake turn brownish in tint.

⅓ cup (80 milliliters) vegetable oil,
plus more for greasing the pan

¾ cup (180 milliliters) hot water

1½ tablespoons green tea powder (*matcha* or *garu nokcha*)

2 cups (230 grams) cake flour

1 tablespoon baking powder

½ teaspoon kosher salt or sea salt

7 large eggs, separated

1 cup (200 grams) superfine sugar

Chantilly Cream:

2 tablespoons confectioners' sugar

1 cup (240 milliliters) heavy cream

1 vanilla bean, split lengthwise

PREHEAT THE OVEN to 350°F.

Lightly brush just the bottom of an angel food cake mold with oil. Do not oil the sides. Set aside. In a heatproof bowl or cup, combine the hot water and matcha, stir until the matcha has dissolved, then let cool to room temperature.

In a small bowl, whisk together the flour, baking powder, and salt; set aside. In a large bowl, beat the egg whites and 3 tablespoons of the superfine sugar with an electric mixer on high speed until medium-stiff peaks form; set aside. In a separate large bowl, beat the egg yolks and remaining superfine sugar on high speed until pale yellow and fluffy. Reduce the speed to low and add the green tea in a slow and steady stream down the side of the bowl, mixing until completely incorporated. Add the oil in the same manner and mix until completely incorporated.

In three additions, gently fold the flour mixture into the yolk mixture. When all the flour mixture has been incorporated, repeat with the egg white mixture, taking care not to overmix. Pour the batter into the prepared cake mold and bake for about 50 minutes, rotating about halfway through, until a toothpick inserted into the center comes out clean. Invert the mold onto a wire rack and without unmolding, let the cake cool completely.

WHEN THE CAKE IS ALMOST READY TO BE SERVED, MAKE THE CHANTILLY CREAM: Put the sugar in a large bowl and pour the cream on top. Scrape the seeds from the vanilla bean into the bowl and then beat the mixture with a hand mixer on medium-high speed until soft peaks form, taking care not to overbeat.

Run a thin knife around the sides and center of the cake mold and then turn the cake out onto a platter. Slice with a serrated knife and serve with the Chantilly cream.

TIP: *You can substitute other flavorings for the green tea, such as espresso powder, citrus juice, or a few dashes of vanilla extract. Just keep the total amount of liquid the same. And instead of Chantilly cream, try serving the cake with fresh fruit, fruit purees, custard, or chocolate sauce.*

# NEW YORK–STYLE CHEESECAKE

*WITH CITRON TEA*

**MAKES ONE 8-INCH CAKE**

I don't know if there's a dessert more synonymous with the Big Apple than New York–style cheesecake—rich, creamy, and mile-high. To balance the decadence a bit, I top it with *yujacha*, a sweet and slightly bitter citron tea syrup.

2½ tablespoons (45 grams) unsalted butter, melted, plus more for greasing the pan

1 cup (105 grams) graham cracker crumbs (from about 7 sheets of crackers; see Tip)

1 pound (452 grams) cream cheese, at room temperature

1 cup (213 grams) sugar

6 large egg yolks

2 teaspoons vanilla extract

3 cups (680 grams) sour cream

3 tablespoons fresh lemon juice

¼ teaspoon kosher salt or sea salt

¼ cup plus 3 tablespoons (125 grams) citron tea syrup (*yujacha*)

**PREHEAT THE OVEN** to 350°F. Grease an 8-inch springform pan with butter. To prevent seepage of water into the pan, set it in the center of a large sheet of heavy-duty aluminum foil (or a double layer of regular foil) and scrunch the foil all around the sides up to right underneath the top rim.

Bring a large pot of water to a boil over high heat; remove from the heat once it boils. Meanwhile, in a medium bowl, mix together the graham cracker crumbs and melted butter with a fork until the mixture resembles wet sand. Press the mixture firmly and evenly into the bottom of the prepared pan with the bottom of a measuring cup or glass. Transfer the pan to the freezer until the filling is ready.

In a large bowl, beat the cream cheese and sugar with an electric mixer on medium speed until smooth, about 30 seconds. Scrape down the sides of the bowl with a rubber spatula. In a medium bowl, beat the yolks and vanilla with a whisk or fork. Working in two batches, add the yolk mixture to the cream cheese mixture and beat on medium speed until combined, scraping down the bowl between additions. Scrape down the sides of the bowl again. Add the sour cream, lemon juice, and salt and beat on medium speed until smooth, about 30 seconds, taking care not to overmix.

Set the springform pan in a sturdy deep roasting pan, scrape the cream cheese mixture over the graham cracker crust, and smooth the top. Carefully pour the hot water into the roasting pan until it reaches halfway up the sides of the springform pan. Carefully transfer the roasting pan to the oven and bake for 45 minutes. Turn off the oven and let the cake cool for 1 hour without opening the door.

Remove the roasting pan from the oven. The cheesecake should be barely golden and still slightly jiggly in the center. Carefully transfer the springform pan to a wire rack and discard the foil. Run a thin knife around the sides of the pan to help prevent the cake from splitting as it cools. Let cool to room temperature, about 1½ hours. Loosely cover the top of the pan with foil without touching the top of the cake and refrigerate until set, at least 6 hours.

To serve, release and remove the sides of the pan. Smooth the sides of the cake with a warmed knife or offset spatula, if necessary. Carefully spread an even layer of the citron tea syrup on top of the cake and then dip a knife into hot water and cut the cake into slices, rinsing the knife in hot water and drying it after each cut.

TIP: *To make graham cracker crumbs, break the crackers into smaller pieces and place in a resealable plastic bag. Use a rolling pin to crush the crackers into fine crumbs. Alternatively, you can pulse the crackers in a food processor.*

# CITRON TEA POSSET

**SERVES 4 TO 6**

Unless you're familiar with British cuisine, you may not have heard of the dessert posset. The best way to describe it is a cream-based lemon pudding. I top it with thinned citron tea syrup (*yujacha*), which is made from the Asian citrus fruit, *yuja* (in Japanese it is called *yuzu*), and has a delightful floral fragrance and bitter-lemon marmalade-like flavor that cuts through the sweetness of the posset really well.

I like to zest the lemon on a Microplane so it's very fine. If your tool results in larger bits of zest, you may wish to pass the flavored cream mixture through a fine-mesh strainer before pouring it into serving glasses.

1¾ cups (420 milliliters) heavy cream

½ cup (100 grams) sugar

Grated zest and juice of 1 lemon

2 tablespoons citron tea syrup (*yujacha*)

Crystallized Lemon Zest (page 261),
for serving (optional)

IN A MEDIUM saucepan, combine the cream and sugar and gently simmer, stirring often, until the sugar has dissolved, about 3 minutes. Remove from the heat and let cool until warm.

Whisk the lemon zest and juice into the cooled cream mixture. Pour into four to six serving glasses (I like to use martini glasses), small bowls, or ramekins, cover each with plastic wrap, and refrigerate until set, about 3 hours.

Before serving, in a very small bowl, stir together the citron tea syrup and 1 tablespoon water. Spoon the liquid on top of each posset, swirling the glass so the top is evenly coated. Top with crystallized lemon zest, if desired.

TIP: *A nice alternative is to flavor the posset with* omija-cha, *five-flavor berry tea, instead of* yujacha. *Omija are small red berries that have five flavors: sweet, sour, salty, bitter, and spicy. The tea can be difficult to find, but it's worth your while to search for it.*

# SEAWEED SHORTBREAD

**MAKES ABOUT THIRTY 3 x ¾-INCH PIECES**

It may seem odd to put seaweed in cookies, but trust me, the mix of savory, slightly briny, sweet, and buttery somehow works and is used in many Asian sweets. The type of seaweed to look for is *kimjaban*. Generally used as a topping for rice or noodles, it's seasoned (usually with sesame oil, sugar, and salt), roasted, and shredded or crumbled. To finely crush them, put the *kimjaban* in a plastic bag and roll them with a rolling pin. If you have sheets of seasoned roasted seaweed (*kim*), though, you can use those, too. Just chop them before using.

2 cups plus 2 tablespoons (250 grams) all-purpose flour

½ cup (80 grams) rice flour

¼ teaspoon kosher salt or sea salt

½ cup plus 2 tablespoons (16 grams) shredded or crumbled seasoned roasted seaweed (*kimjaban*), finely crushed

1 cup (2 sticks/227 grams) unsalted butter, cut into cubes, at room temperature

½ cup (100 grams) superfine sugar, plus more for sprinkling

1 large egg, lightly beaten with a splash of water (egg wash)

½ teaspoon flaky sea salt, such as Maldon

PREHEAT THE OVEN to 300°F. Line a 9-inch square baking pan with parchment paper, letting some paper overhang on opposite sides to act as handles; set aside.

Combine the all-purpose flour, rice flour, and kosher salt in a sifter and sift into a large bowl. Whisk in ½ cup of the seaweed and set aside.

In a large bowl, beat the butter with an electric mixer on medium speed until fluffy, 1½ to 2 minutes. Scrape down the sides of the bowl with a rubber spatula, add the sugar, and beat on high speed until creamy, about 2 minutes. Add the flour mixture and beat on low until the dough resembles wet sand and holds together when squeezed. Press evenly into the prepared pan. Bake for 1 hour and 20 minutes until light golden. Set the baking pan on a wire rack and let cool for 5 minutes. Leave the oven on.

Using the parchment paper as handles, lift the shortbread out of the pan and transfer to a cutting board. Cut the shortbread (while on the paper) into thirds and then into roughly ¾-inch-wide pieces. Brush the tops lightly with the egg wash and sprinkle with some sugar, the remaining 2 tablespoons seaweed, and flaky sea salt. Transfer the pieces to a baking sheet and spread them out so they're not touching. Bake for 10 minutes, so the sides dry out a bit, and then set aside until cool. Store in an airtight container.

# JUJUBE BAR COOKIES

### MAKES ABOUT 72 COOKIES

This is my take on the Sicilian fig cookies called *cuccidati*, which are a fancier version of that classic American childhood fave, Fig Newtons. Everyone I give these cookies to loves them wholly. I am sure you will find many fans as well. To give it an Asian flair, I swap in jujubes (*daechu*) for the figs, plum wine for the brandy, and *yujacha*, citron tea syrup, for the orange marmalade. Jujubes are dried Chinese red dates, which are from a different family than the dates from the palm family (i.e., Deglet Noor and Medjool). They are mild flavored, not very sweet, and contain a small pit. Don't be tempted to purchase them already pitted, as they lose flavor once the seeds are removed.

Filling:

¾ cup (116 grams) whole almonds, toasted and chopped

¾ cup (92 grams) walnut pieces, toasted

¼ cup (33 grams) pine nuts, toasted

1½ teaspoons ground cinnamon

⅛ teaspoon freshly grated nutmeg

Pinch of kosher salt or sea salt

12 ounces (341 grams) jujube dates (*daechu*), pitted and coarsely chopped

¾ cup (112 grams) golden raisins

⅓ cup (80 milliliters) plum wine

¾ cup (242 grams) citron tea syrup (*yujacha*)

Dough:

1 large egg

½ cup (118 milliliters) whole milk

1 tablespoon vanilla extract

4 cups (482 grams) all-purpose flour, plus more for dusting

¾ cup (162 grams) granulated sugar

4 teaspoons baking powder

½ teaspoon kosher salt or sea salt

1 cup (2 sticks/227 grams) unsalted butter, cut into cubes, at room temperature

1 large egg white, lightly beaten with a splash of water

½ cup (50 grams) sliced unblanched almonds

Raw sugar or Demerara sugar (optional)

FOR THE FILLING: In a food processor, combine the almonds, walnuts, pine nuts, cinnamon, nutmeg, and salt and pulse until pebbly. Don't pulse too long, or the mixture will turn into a nut butter. Transfer to a bowl and set aside. Put the dates and raisins in the food processor and pulse until coarsely chopped. Add the plum wine and citron tea syrup and process until a coarse paste forms. Add the nut mixture and process until relatively smooth, but still a little pebbly. Transfer the filling to a medium bowl, cover, and refrigerate for 4 hours or overnight so the flavors can develop.

Jujube Bar Cookies and Korean
Coffee Brownies (page 253)

FOR THE DOUGH: In a small bowl, whisk together the egg, milk, and vanilla and set aside. In the bowl of a stand mixer fitted with the paddle attachment, mix together the flour, granulated sugar, baking powder, and salt on low speed. Gradually add the butter and mix until crumbly, about 2 minutes. Slowly pour in the egg mixture and mix until a smooth dough forms, about 3 minutes. Gather the dough into a ball, wrap tightly in plastic wrap, and let rest in the refrigerator for 45 minutes.

Preheat the oven to 350°F. Line two baking sheets with parchment paper.

Let the dough warm up a little and then divide it in half. Put one half on a lightly floured work surface and rewrap the other. Roll the dough into a 12 x 15-inch rectangle about ¼ inch thick. Trim the edges and cut the rectangle crosswise into thirds (you should have three even rectangles).

Divide the filling evenly into six portions, then roll each into a log about 12 inches long. Working in batches, put one log in the middle of one piece of dough and gently press down to flatten it slightly so the log is ½ inch tall by 1 inch wide. Fold the long sides of the pastry over the log and arrange it so it's seam-side down. Transfer to the baking sheet. Repeat with the remaining dough and filling, putting a total of three encased logs on each baking sheet.

Brush the tops with the egg white and sprinkle with the sliced almonds and raw sugar (if using). Bake for 25 to 30 minutes, rotating the pans halfway through, until just lightly golden. Let the logs cool slightly and then transfer to a cutting board. While they're still warm, cut them crosswise into 1-inch pieces and let cool a little more or to room temperature before serving. Completely cooled cookies can be stored in an airtight container.

TIP: *If you like these cookies with a soft exterior, put them in a single layer in a container with a tight-fitting lid while still warm and cover. (They can be stored in layers when they are completely cooled.)*

# KOREAN COFFEE BROWNIES

### MAKES SIXTEEN 2-INCH SQUARES

When it comes to brownies, people either fall into the chewy-fudgy camp or the cakey camp. The way I see it, if you want chocolate cake, you might as well make chocolate cake. These brownies are so dense and rich that you only need one square with a cold glass of milk, but you can also go all-out and top it with a scoop of Caramel Doenjang Ice Cream (page 235) or any ice cream you like.

Coffee brings out the best in chocolate, so I like to add Korean instant coffee, which comes in individual packets complete with creamer and sugar, to my brownies. This recipe is really quick and easy and only requires one mixing bowl and a wooden spoon or rubber spatula, so you have no excuse to buy boxed brownie mix ever again.

---

8 tablespoons (1 stick/113 grams) unsalted butter, plus more for greasing the pan

4 ounces (113 grams) unsweetened chocolate, coarsely chopped

3 (⅜-ounce) packets Korean instant coffee (36 grams or about ¼ cup total)

1½ cups (338 grams) sugar

1 tablespoon vanilla extract

¼ teaspoon kosher salt or sea salt

2 large eggs, at room temperature

1 cup (122 grams) all-purpose flour

2 tablespoons natural cocoa powder (not Dutch-processed)

PREHEAT THE OVEN to 350°F. Grease an 8-inch square pan with butter, line the bottom with parchment paper cut to fit, and then grease the parchment.

In the top of a double boiler over simmering water, heat the butter, chocolate, and coffee, stirring occasionally, until the butter and chocolate have melted and the mixture is smooth. Remove from the heat and let the mixture cool slightly. Beat in the sugar, vanilla, and salt with a wooden spoon or spatula. The mixture will look grainy, but don't worry, it will come together later. Beat in the eggs, one at a time, beating well after each addition. Add the flour and cocoa and beat for a full minute.

Scrape the batter into the prepared pan, smooth the top, and bake for about 30 minutes (if using a metal pan), until a toothpick inserted into the center comes out with a few moist crumbs clinging to it. It will take a little longer if using a glass or ceramic pan.

Set the pan on a wire rack until cool enough to handle, about 45 minutes. Run a thin knife around the sides and then invert the pan onto a large plate or cutting board and peel off the parchment from the bottom of the released brownie. Flip the brownie back onto the rack to cool completely. Cut into 2-inch squares on a cutting board with a sharp knife.

# SESAME AND CANDIED GINGER CRUNCH

## *KKAE GANGJEONG*

**MAKES ABOUT TWENTY-FIVE 1½-INCH PIECES**

Sesame crunch is a nutty candy that makes an appearance in many cultures, including Korea. Growing up in the States, I bought them individually wrapped from bins alongside caramels and other candies. I like them just as much now as I did then, but when I make them I tend to gild the lily, adding candied ginger and dipping them in chocolate. One of the keys to good sesame crunch is to use very fresh sesame seeds. Sesame seeds can easily turn rancid, so be sure to taste them before you start the recipe. I usually buy them already roasted for the sake of convenience, but for this recipe, I toast them myself.

1 cup (130 grams) raw sesame seeds

¼ cup (75 grams) honey

¼ cup (55 grams) sugar

Pinch of kosher salt or sea salt

2 tablespoons chopped candied ginger

½ teaspoon flaky sea salt, such as Maldon

4 ounces (113 grams) bittersweet chocolate, chopped (optional)

PUT THE SESAME seeds in a large heavy skillet. Turn the heat to medium and toast, stirring occasionally, until the seeds are golden and starting to pop, about 8 minutes. Transfer to a plate and let cool.

Top a cutting board with a sheet of parchment paper and set aside. In a large heavy-bottomed skillet, combine the honey, sugar, kosher salt, and 1 tablespoon water and simmer, without stirring but swirling the skillet occasionally, until golden brown, about 5 minutes.

Using a heatproof spatula, stir in the sesame seeds and evenly coat. The mixture will be clumpy. Spread it on the parchment paper and cover with another sheet of parchment paper. Using a rolling pin, flatten the sesame mixture into a ¼-inch-thick square or rectangle. Uncover, top with the ginger and flaky sea salt, cover again, and gently roll to press in the ginger. Set the sesame crunch aside until slightly warm. Cut into 1½-inch pieces using a sharp, lightly greased knife and then let cool completely.

If desired, melt the chocolate in the top of a double boiler over simmering water, stirring occasionally, until smooth. Dip the bottom half of each piece of sesame crunch into the chocolate, letting any excess chocolate drip off. Transfer to a piece of parchment paper to set. When the chocolate has hardened, store the sesame crunch between layers of parchment paper in an airtight container.

# SALTED CARAMEL PANCAKES

## *HOTTEOK*

**MAKES ABOUT TEN 4-INCH PANCAKES**

*Hotteok*, sweet pancakes filled with a brown sugar syrup and nuts, are beloved by young and old alike. These decadent treats were my sister Sonya's choice dessert when we were kids. In each bite, you crunch through a crispy golden crust, then through a chewy dough, and finally into a gooey center. I've jazzed up the classic recipe by substituting the brown sugar with muscovado sugar, which is richer and "oozier" when melted, and mixing it with a touch of salt. Feel free to make your own version as well—I've seen these pancakes filled with everything from walnuts and honey to mixed seeds. And they're even better with a scoop of vanilla ice cream and/or whipped cream on top.

Dough:

**1½ cups (360 milliliters) whole milk**

**2 tablespoons granulated sugar**

**1 packet (7 grams) instant yeast**

**1½ cups (225 grams) bread flour, plus more for dusting**

**1 cup (150 grams) sweet rice flour**

**1½ tablespoons cornstarch**

**½ teaspoon kosher salt or sea salt**

Filling:

**½ cup (125 grams) firmly packed muscovado sugar**

**½ cup (75 grams) peanuts, coarsely chopped**

**1 tablespoon ground cinnamon**

**¾ teaspoon kosher salt or sea salt**

**Vegetable oil, for frying**

FOR THE DOUGH: In a very small saucepan, heat the milk to about 105°F. Remove from the heat, add the sugar and yeast, and whisk until they have dissolved. Let stand in a warm place for 3 to 5 minutes, or until bubbling, to activate the yeast.

In a large bowl, combine the bread flour, rice flour, cornstarch, and salt. Slowly stir in the warm milk mixture until a sticky dough forms. Shape the dough into a ball in the bottom of the bowl and cover the bowl with a clean damp kitchen towel. Let the dough rise in a warm place until doubled in size, 1½ to 2 hours. Punch it down and let it rise until doubled in size again, about 1½ hours more.

FOR THE FILLING: Meanwhile, in a small bowl, mix together the muscovado sugar, peanuts, cinnamon, and salt.

After the dough has risen a second time, dust a clean work surface with flour and turn the dough out onto it. Dust the top of the dough with some more flour and knead it a few times. Shape the dough into a fat, long log.

Cut the dough into ten equal pieces, shape each

piece into a ball, set on the floured work surface, and cover with a clean kitchen towel or plastic wrap. Dusting with flour as needed to prevent sticking, press a dough ball into a 4-inch-wide disc using your fingertips. Make sure the disc is uniformly thick so the finished pancake will be evenly filled with caramel.

Put the disc in your hand and slightly cup it. Spoon 1½ to 2 tablespoons of the filling into the center of the disc. Seal the disc closed by wrapping the dough around the filling and pinching the edges together at the top. Once sealed, reshape gently to form a ball, set with the seam side down on the floured work surface, and cover with a clean kitchen towel or plastic wrap. Repeat with the remaining dough balls and filling.

In a large nonstick skillet, heat 3 tablespoons of oil over medium-high heat. Put two or three dough balls seam-side down in the skillet and immediately flatten them with a spatula to a width of about 4 inches. Reduce the heat to medium-low and fry the pancakes until golden brown and crispy on the bottom, 3 to 4 minutes. Flip them and cook until slightly springy to the touch, 3 to 4 minutes more.

Transfer the pancakes to a wire rack or paper towel–lined plate when done. Repeat with the remaining dough balls, wiping the skillet clean and adding fresh oil for each batch. Let the pancakes cool slightly before serving. It's easy to burn yourself in your haste to gobble these up, as the insides are hot and oozing.

TIP: *If you can't find muscovado sugar, use dark brown sugar. The pancakes will still be delicious.*

# SUGAR AND RED BEAN RAISED DOUGHNUTS

**MAKES 16 TO 18 DOUGHNUTS**

You'll find red bean doughnuts or bread in most Korean pastry shops. Red bean paste often comes in cans in smooth and chunky options, but if all you can find is the latter, you can puree it in a food processor until smooth, if you like. A light dusting of sugar on the doughnut is the perfect finishing touch.

¼ cup (59 milliliters) whole milk

2½ cups (300 grams) all-purpose flour, plus more for beating and dusting

1 tablespoon sugar, plus more as needed for rolling

1½ teaspoons kosher salt or sea salt

1 teaspoon instant yeast

3 large eggs, lightly beaten

4 tablespoons (½ stick/57 grams) unsalted butter, cut into cubes, at room temperature

¾ cup (270 grams) red bean paste

Vegetable oil, for frying

IN A VERY small saucepan, heat the milk to about 105°F. In the bowl of a stand mixer fitted with the dough hook, mix the flour, sugar, salt, and yeast on low speed. Add the eggs and warmed milk and beat on medium speed until a smooth but sticky ball of dough forms, about 5 minutes. With the mixer running on low speed, add the butter piece by piece, waiting for each piece to be incorporated before adding the next, until the dough completely pulls away from the sides of the bowl and becomes very smooth and supple, 8 to 10 minutes more. Shape the dough into a ball, transfer to a lightly greased bowl, and cover with a clean kitchen towel or plastic wrap. Set in a warm spot and let rise until doubled in size, about 2 hours.

Line a baking sheet with parchment paper and set aside. Transfer the dough to a lightly floured work surface and roll out to a thickness of ¼ inch. Using a 2½-inch round cutter, cut out as many discs as you can and then cover the dough with a clean kitchen towel or plastic wrap.

Take two discs, which will likely have contracted slightly, and stretch each one back to a diameter of 2½ inches, if needed. Put 2 teaspoons of the red bean paste in the center of one disc. Cover with the other disc and tightly pinch and flatten the edges together, stretching the dough to a diameter of 3 inches. Using the cutter, cut the filled dough-nut, twisting the cutter as you push down to seal the edges. Transfer the doughnut to the prepared baking sheet and lightly cover with a clean kitchen towel or plastic wrap. Repeat the process with the remaining dough discs and red bean paste.

Gather the dough scraps into a ball and roll out one more time. Cut out as many discs as you can. (If the rerolled dough is very elastic, first wrap it in plastic wrap and set aside for 10 to 15 minutes to let it relax.) Repeat the stretching, filling, and cutting process with the discs and the remaining red bean paste. Once all the doughnuts are formed, set the baking sheet in a warm spot and let the doughnuts rise until they are doubled in size, about 30 minutes.

When the doughnuts are almost ready, pour some sugar into a shallow bowl and set aside. In a large, wide, heavy-bottomed pot at least 5 inches deep, heat 2 inches of oil over medium-high heat until it reaches 375°F. Working in batches of three or four, gently slip the doughnuts into the oil and fry, turning and submerging them occasionally with a slotted spoon, until deep golden brown and nicely puffed, about 2 minutes. Transfer to a wire rack or paper towel–lined plate to drain. Let the oil return to 375°F between batches.

Lightly roll the doughnuts in sugar, knocking off any excess. They are best eaten when still slightly warm.

TIP: *Try to cut as many discs as possible from the first rolling of the dough because the rerolled dough won't rise as much. Any remaining scraps can be formed into small balls and fried.*

# CRYSTALLIZED LEMON ZEST

**MAKES ABOUT 2 TABLESPOONS**

If possible, use organic lemons. Otherwise, be sure to scrub the lemons really well. If you don't have superfine sugar, regular granulated sugar will work in a pinch. This recipe works with any citrus fruit.

2 large lemons

3 tablespoons superfine sugar

**RUN A FOUR-PRONG** curly lemon zester from one end of each lemon to the other to create long, thin strips of zest, working your way all the way around the fruit. On a large plate, toss together the zest and sugar. Spread the zest out in a single layer and let dry for about 30 minutes, tossing occasionally. Store in an airtight container. Tap off any excess sugar before using.

# DRINKS

# ROASTED BARLEY TEA

*BORICHA*

**SERVES 6**

*Boricha*, a nutty, caffeine-free tisane, is made with unhulled, roasted barley that is simmered in a pot of water. When I was a kid, my mom used loose barley and I loved to fish out the "cooked" grains from the bottom of the pot and eat them. If you're feeling lazy, nowadays it's easy to find the barley in tea bags. You can brew it in a pot, or, for a lighter *boricha*, put it in a cup and pour boiling water over it.

Combining barley with the corn used in Roasted Corn Tea (page 265) is also nice, as it lends sweetness. If you'd like to try it, use half barley and half corn.

**8 cups cold water, preferably spring water**

**½ cup unhulled roasted barley**

IN A MEDIUM SAUCEPAN, combine the water and barley and bring to a boil over high heat. Reduce the heat to maintain a simmer for 20 minutes. Pass the tea through a fine-mesh strainer, discard the solids, and serve hot or cold (see Variation, below).

**VARIATION:**

**Iced Barley Tea**
*Iced Boricha*

*At Korean restaurants, instead of glasses of water, you are often presented with iced barley tea. It's very refreshing, especially when paired with spicy dishes. The tea is diluted with icy cold water so that there's just a hint of barley flavor. At home, you can make it light like at the restaurants or just chill regular-strength brewed tea. If you're using barley tea bags, you can also make it like sun tea or just throw a couple of tea bags in a pitcher of water and let it steep in the fridge until you've achieved the desired strength.*

# ROASTED CORN TEA
## *OKSUSUCHA*

**SERVES 8**

The corn roasted for tea is not the same as the sweet, juicy corn we eat in the States. Rather, it's glutinous, starchy, and chewy and has a very mild flavor. This Korean corn is an acquired taste if you didn't grow up with it. As with Roasted Barley Tea (page 264), you can brew loose roasted corn kernels (found in the tea section of Asian markets, often next to the roasted barley) in a pot or steep tea bags in hot water. Corn tea is also caffeine-free.

**10 cups cold water, preferably spring water**

**½ cup roasted corn kernels**

IN A MEDIUM SAUCEPAN, combine the water and corn and bring to a boil over high heat. Reduce the heat to maintain a simmer for 20 minutes. Pass the tea through a fine-mesh stainer, discard the solids, and serve hot or cold.

# RICE PUNCH

## *SIKHYE*

**SERVES 4 TO 6**

*Sikhye* is a lightly fermented and sweet cold beverage made by fermenting cooked rice in a barley malt powder liquid. My mom used to make this by the bucketful, and our laundry room was full of huge jars of this milky liquid. Instead of flavoring it with the traditional ginger and/or dried red dates (jujubes), I prefer a plump vanilla bean.

This recipe is a great way to use up leftover rice, but if you're making a fresh batch, cut back on the water a little so that it comes out a little drier.

---

10 cups cold water, preferably spring water

1 cup barley malt powder (*yeot gireum*)

2 cups Steamed White Rice (page 106), chilled or at room temperature

¾ cup sugar, plus more to taste

1 vanilla bean, split lengthwise

Pine nuts, for serving

---

IN A LARGE BOWL, stir together the water and malt powder and then let soak for about 2 hours. The malt powder will sink to the bottom of the bowl.

After the malt powder has soaked, in a slow cooker or rice cooker with a "warm" function, stir together the rice and ½ cup of the sugar. (If you don't have a cooker, combine the rice and sugar in a medium ovenproof saucepan and preheat the oven to 200°F.)

Without stirring up the sludgy malt powder sediment, ladle the liquid at the top of the bowl into the rice mixture. Stop when you reach the sediment. Mix well, cover the cooker, and turn on the "warm" function. (If you're using a saucepan, cover it and put it in the oven.) Let sit until a few grains of rice float to the surface, 4 to 5 hours. (This is to ferment the rice.)

Pass the rice mixture through a fine-mesh strainer into a large saucepan, reserving the rice. Add the remaining ¼ cup sugar to the saucepan and bring the liquid to a boil over high heat, stirring until the sugar has dissolved. Reduce the heat to maintain a simmer, skimming off any foam, for about 10 minutes. Scrape the vanilla bean seeds into the saucepan, add the pod, and stir. Taste and add more sugar, if you like. Set aside to cool to room temperature and then refrigerate until very cold.

Meanwhile, rinse the reserved rice under cold water, drain, and store separately in the refrigerator. To serve, spoon the punch into cups or bowls, add a spoonful of rice to each, and top with a couple pine nuts.

# CINNAMON AND PERSIMMON PUNCH

## *SUJEONGGWA*

**MAKES 8 CUPS; SERVES 8**

Cinnamon sticks, fresh ginger, and dried persimmons are the base for this deliciously fragrant, sweet, and spicy punch. While this "digestif" is often served during the Lunar New Year and Moon Festival celebrations, it's easy enough to make a big batch to stash in the fridge for a daily swig. This can be served hot or cold, but I prefer it icy cold. I also like to make it into Cinnamon and Persimmon Punch Sorbet (page 234).

---

**10 cups water**

**12 cinnamon sticks, rinsed**

**½ cup thinly sliced peeled fresh ginger (from an 8-inch knob; about 3 ounces)**

**⅔ cup tightly packed brown sugar**

**4 dried persimmons (*gotgam*), stems removed**

**Ice, for serving**

**Pine nuts, for garnish**

ADD THE WATER, cinnamon, and ginger, to a large pot. Bring to a boil over high heat, then reduce the heat to maintain a simmer. Partially cover and simmer for 40 minutes. Add the sugar and stir until it has dissolved, then remove from the heat. Strain through a fine-mesh strainer into a large bowl or pitcher and add the persimmons. Set aside to cool to room temperature, then cover and refrigerate until well chilled, at least 2 hours.

To serve, pour the punch over ice in bowls or cups and garnish with pine nuts. The soaked persimmons can also be sliced or left whole as a garnish, if you like.

---

TIP: *Look for soft, plump, dried persimmons in the produce section of Korean markets. They are often packaged tightly wrapped in plastic wrap on Styrofoam trays.*

# SOJU INFUSIONS

I have to thank my talented bar manager, Kristian Breivik, for his creative takes on soju below, and the cocktails to follow in the next pages. At Jinjuu, our soju cocktails and infusions complete our contemporary Korean menu. I am a massive fan of Hwayo Soju, as it is only made from rice and water. If you cannot find this particular brand, Jinro is a great substitute as well.

The following three infusions can be chilled and taken as shots or used to make the other cocktails in this section. The recipes can be scaled up or down as desired.

### CELERY AND BLACK PEPPER SOJU INFUSION

Fill a 1½-liter jar with a tight-fitting lid halfway with 2-inch-long celery sticks. Add 3 tablespoons whole black peppercorns and fill the jar with soju. Cover and let sit at room temperature for at least a day and up to a week, making sure the soju covers the celery. Keep refrigerated. Strain before serving.

### LYCHEE SOJU INFUSION

Fill a 1½-liter jar with a tight-fitting lid two-thirds of the way with peeled and pitted fresh lychees. (Drained canned lychees will work in a pinch.) Fill the jar with soju, cover, and let sit at room temperature for at least a day and up to a week, making sure the soju covers the fruit. Keep refrigerated. Strain before serving.

### RED PLUM SOJU INFUSION

Fill a 1½-liter jar with a tight-fitting lid halfway with halved pitted unpeeled red plums. Fill the jar with soju, cover, and let sit at room temperature for at least a day and up to a week, making sure the soju covers the fruit. Keep refrigerated. Strain before serving.

# SPICED KIMCHI MARY

**MAKES 1 DRINK**

We literally cannot make this drink fast enough to keep up with the demand. It flies off the bar, and customers say it is the best Bloody Mary in town. It's making my bar manager, the inventor, Kristian Breivik, quite famous. It goes particularly well with our Roasted Pork Belly Lettuce Wraps (page 200) as a Korean take on the classic Sunday roast.

Lime wedge

*Gochugaru* (Korean chile flakes)

Ice, for serving

7 tablespoons tomato juice

¼ cup Spicy Kimchi Mix (right)

¼ cup Celery and Black Pepper Soju Infusion (page 269)

1 celery stick, for serving

Shrimp chips (optional)

RUB THE LIME wedge around the outside rim of a tall glass and then roll the rim of the glass in the chile flakes. Fill the glass with ice. Combine the tomato juice, kimchi mix, and soju infusion in the glass and stir for 10 seconds. Garnish with the celery stick. Serve shrimp chips alongside for snacking, if you'd like.

## SPICY KIMCHI MIX

**MAKES ABOUT ¼ CUP PLUS 2 TEASPOONS**

5 teaspoons kimchi juice from Cabbage Kimchi (page 28) or jarred kimchi base

5 teaspoons tomato cocktail with clam juice, preferably Clamato

2 teaspoons Sriracha sauce or other hot sauce or chile sauce

1 teaspoon *gochujang* (Korean chile paste)

1 teaspoon fresh lime juice

IN A SMALL BOWL, stir together all the ingredients.

# LYCHEE LOVER

**MAKES 1 DRINK**

The ever-popular lychee takes center stage here with its fragrant sweet notes and alluring pinkish hue. A little bubbly, either Champagne or prosecco, makes this cocktail festive, and it is a perfect way to make any party feel a bit more luxurious. The infused lychee soju is great on its own as well, served chilled.

**7 teaspoons Lychee Soju Infusion (page 269)**

**5 teaspoons lychee liqueur**

**2 teaspoons fresh lime juice**

**2 ounces sparkling wine**

**1 strip lemon peel, for garnish (optional)**

**1 peeled and pitted lychee, preferably fresh, for garnish (optional)**

COMBINE THE SOJU infusion, lychee liqueur, and lime juice in a cocktail shaker filled with ice and shake hard for 10 seconds. Strain into a champagne flute and top with the sparkling wine. Garnish with the lemon peel and/or lychee.

# THE PSY SOUR

## MAKES 1 DRINK

Look for Korean ginseng drink with honey in Korean markets. It usually comes in small clear bottles; the most popular brand is Royal King. If you cannot find it, Honey Syrup (right) is a good substitute. *Yuja*, an Asian citron fruit, is called *yuzu* in Japanese and is available at Japanese markets. Lemon juice will do in a pinch. We serve ours with a ginseng candy and a traditional Hwatu playing card.

7 teaspoons 41% soju, preferably Hwayo

5 teaspoons *yuja* juice or fresh lemon juice

1 tablespoon Kamm & Sons Ginseng Spirit

1 tablespoon Korean ginseng drink with honey or Honey Syrup (right)

1 large egg white

Dash of lavender bitters (optional)

1 strip lemon peel, for garnish (optional)

1 piece ginseng candy, for garnish (optional)

COMBINE THE SOJU, *yuja* juice, ginseng spirit, ginseng drink, egg white, and bitters in a cocktail shaker and shake for 10 seconds. Fill the shaker with ice and shake hard for 15 seconds more. Strain into a cocktail glass and garnish with the lemon peel and/or ginseng candy, if desired. Drink the cocktail before and after eating the ginseng candy to experience the difference in flavor.

## HONEY SYRUP

### MAKES ABOUT 4 TEASPOONS

2½ teaspoons honey

1½ teaspoons hot water

IN A SMALL BOWL, stir together the honey and hot water until the honey has dissolved.

# JINJUULEP

**MAKES 1 DRINK**

This Korean twist on a classic julep, served at my restaurant, Jinjuu, swaps out mint in favor of peppery perilla leaves. The plum soju also adds a great undertone of stone fruit flavor and welcomed sweetness. I like to serve it in a clear glass to show off the gorgeous leaves.

**6 large perilla leaves (*ggaennip*), also known as sesame leaves**

**8 teaspoons blended Scotch whisky**

**7 teaspoons Red Plum Soju Infusion (page 269)**

**1 tablespoon Simple Syrup (right)**

**Confectioners' sugar, for garnish**

COMBINE 5 OF THE perilla leaves, the whisky, soju infusion, and simple syrup in a stainless-steel cup and fill halfway with crushed ice. Stir well until frost forms on the cup. Top with crushed ice and garnish with the remaining perilla leaf and a dusting of confectioners' sugar.

## SIMPLE SYRUP

**MAKES ABOUT ⅓ CUP**

**¼ cup sugar**

IN A VERY small saucepan, combine the sugar and ¼ cup water and simmer until the sugar has dissolved. Let cool completely.

# SOJU BOMBS

Soju bombs are one of the most popular drinks in Korean bars. I like to pair them with my Chile Bombs (page 78).

## CLASSIC SOJU BOMB

**MAKES 1 DRINK**

POUR CHILLED SOJU into a shot glass and drop into a glass of cold beer. Chug. If you want to be more specific, use a ratio of 3 parts soju to 7 parts beer.

## COKE, SOJU, AND BEER
*COJINGANMEK*

**MAKES 1 DRINK**

This is a variation on the Classic Soju Bomb. The sweet cola helps with the bitterness.

FILL A SHOT glass with cold Coca-Cola or other cola and set it in a small beer glass. Fill a second shot glass with cold soju and set it atop the shot glass of cola. Fill the glass with cold beer. Chug.

# INDEX